ALL BORN UNDER THE ONE BLUE SKY

Irish people share their adoption stories

Cúnamh

ORIGINAL WRITING

ISBNS
PARENT : 978-1-909007-97-0
EPUB: 978-1-78237-064-2
MOBI: 978-1-78237-065-9
PDF: 978-1-78237-022-2

A CIP catalogue for this book is available from the National Library.

Published by ORIGINAL WRITING LTD., Dublin, 2013.
Printed by CLONDALKIN GROUP, Glasnevin, Dublin 11

This book is dedicated to all those who have come to Cúnamh in the past, who are here presently and for those who may come in the future

FOREWORD

The story of Cúnamh tells us a lot about Ireland since 1913. The early unseemly squabbling between Christian denominations over the right to the loyalty and souls of the poor, the orphaned and the abandoned has overtones that resonate today as progress towards Christian Unity proceeds at a snail's pace. It is a backdrop not without irony for many of the children and families concerned, their lives shaped by a forceful culture of shame around illegitimacy and powerlessness around poverty. The love at the heart of the Christian gospel had to work on stony soil. But work it did and in its special vocation of care for fostered and adopted children and their birth and adoptive families, Cúnamh, like them, like our country, grew up, grew older and wiser, so that today the services it offers have a deep level of sensitivity and profound insight that draws from wells of often bitter and yet somehow also joyful experience. Who filled those wells with their tears both of joy and sorrow, with their hopes and dreams? The children whose lives are chronicled here and their birth parents, their adoptive and foster families whose lives were all radically altered by events that brought them into Cúnamh's orbit. Through them, and through a new secular consciousness of the rights of the individual, our country thankfully abandoned the appalling notion of illegitimacy and began to look more acutely at the rights of children and in particular the rights of adopted children. Who can tell what is in their hearts? Only they can, and with the help of welcome this centenary chronicles, they offer to us a view of the world we need to hear and need to listen to with care. Their birth and adoptive parents open their hearts too. Here are stories from our own families and communities that reveal heartening and heartbreaking depths of resilience, strength and coping skills.

All Born Under The One Blue Sky is a testimony to how people can rise to the challenges they meet. It is a book of Irish adoption stories written by people who in someway have 'lived' adoption. All of the writers have their own perspective, their own story to tell, extraordinary and unique yet the enduring echoes of joy, pain, fear and wonder are recognizable throughout.

This book could not have been completed without the willingness of so many to share openly and honestly their stories. *All Born Under The One Blue Sky* will bring you into the world of the birth mother and the lifelong consequence of the decision she made for her baby. You will experience the joy of new adoptive parents having firstly come to terms with their infertility. You will journey with the adopted person who is searching for answers to breathtakingly big personal questions that just will not go away.

There is, I hope, support and encouragement here for anyone whose life has brought them into similar situations, similar awful dilemmas. It is a privilege to have been asked by Cúnamh to write this foreword, for Cúnamh has given our community great care and service these past one hundred years. At this end of Cúnamh's first century and the start of its second, I say a heartfelt thank you to its staff and funders, those who sought its help, those who opened their lives as foster parents and adoptive parents and especially to the children whose little lives were so dramatically shaped by events and circumstances far beyond their ken or control. Through all of them we can hope to come to know more intimately and humbly the inside story of fostering and adoption, to understand the human condition more keenly and to offer a love that is warm and real, healing and helping.

Professor Mary McAleese

INTRODUCTION

Cúnamh, a registered charity, formerly known as The Catholic Protection and Rescue Society of Ireland (C.P.R.S.I.) first opened its doors in 1913, one hundred years ago. It was founded by a group of lay Catholics due to concerns that Catholic children and their families were being taken care of by Protestant charitable agencies. The purpose of the C.P.R.S.I. was to protect the faith of baptised Catholics in Ireland by providing short-term or long-term care for children and families as well as financial help. The agency first worked from 35 Molesworth Street, Dublin 2 and in 1921 moved to 30 South Anne Street, Dublin 2 where it has been based ever since.

With the introduction of legal adoption in 1952 Cúnamh became a registered adoption agency and this role continues under the Adoption Act 2010. Cúnamh, a voluntary agency, is part-funded by the State and in view of this relies on fundraising, as it has always done, to continue to provide and expand its services.

Prior to 1952 the agency endeavoured to support mothers and families who felt unable or were not in a position to parent their children, by placing these children with Catholic foster families or in Catholic institutions. From the introduction of legal adoption in 1952 until the late seventies the primary role of the agency was to offer help and support to a mother who was considering placing her baby for adoption, to assess and prepare couples for adoptive parenthood and to place babies in permanent and loving homes. Once a child was placed and the adoption order granted, the agency closed the file in the belief that a birth mother, having made her decision, was free to continue with her life and the adoptive family no longer required input from the agency.

However, from the late seventies, there was a growing acknowledgement that the needs of birth parents, adoptive parents and adopted persons were not always met with the granting of the adoption order. Cúnamh has come to recognise that the connection to adoption is life-long and that any or all the parties to the adoption may need to deal with important issues arising from the adoption at different stages over the course of their lives. Cúnamh has responded by expanding its services to provide an ongoing post adoption, counselling, support and information and trace service.

Why the book?

We wished to mark Cúnamh's centenary and thought what better way than to give you, the reader, an insight into the world of Irish adoption. With this in mind we asked those who use our service, birth mothers, birth fathers, adoptive parents, adopted persons and their families, to share their experiences. The response to this request and people's generosity and honesty in sharing such deeply personal experiences was overwhelming. The experiences of Irish people, shaped in someway by adoption, have now been brought together in this compilation of moving stories and poems. Each story will bring the reader along the different paths journeyed by the writers. They will make you laugh, cry and pull at your heart-strings. They are a reminder to us all of the strength of love, the need to belong and the great lengths we will go to find inner peace.

Reading such personal and sensitive stories is a privilege and we sincerely thank each of the writers for sharing their thoughts and feelings in such an open and giving way.

The illustrations seen throughout this book were created by Erin, through her own experience as an adoptive parent and as a direct response to the stories shared within 'All Born Under The One Blue Sky'

Julie Kerins
Secretary/Senior Social Worker

Contents

Adopted persons share their stories

Others share their adoption stories

BIRTH PARENTS SHARE THEIR STORIES

ALL BORN UNDER THE ONE BLUE SKY

All Born Under the One Blue Sky
Some to keep and some to share
But all to continue on their circle of life
Be it with family
Or
Be it to share
All with hope, expectations and care
Moving forward time never stops
Always the sound, the tick, tick of the clock
Decisions made
Can't look back
Moving forward
Under God's Blue Sky
Can't go back and repaint the Sky

Anonymous

GOODBYE LITTLE DARLIN'

So this is goodbye little darlin',
My heart breaks to leave you behind,
And promise me that you will never
Be nobody's darlin' but mine.

I thought the end of the world had come when I said goodbye to my little baby believing I would never see her again. The above was a popular song at that time and it always brings me back to that heart-breaking day. It was 1960's Ireland when attitudes towards pregnancy outside marriage were, to say the least, unchristian. There was little or no support for single mothers, either within the community or in most families. In fact we did not know our rights and to this day I wonder why I did not enquire into them. I was probably too vulnerable and incapable of rational thinking. Usually girls were obliged to resign from work because of the stigma of single pregnancy. Some went to England but others stayed in Ireland, as I did, secreted away some place, so as not to shock the neighbours or society. I had to live the lie that I had emigrated, returning later pretending that emigration was not for me. Giving a child up for adoption is lifelong bereavement through which the birth mother often has to suffer alone. The advice given was to go away and forget!

So commenced more than 40 years of deception, lack of confidence and low self-esteem, together with feelings of deep guilt, shame and grief. I often felt as if I lived in a cocoon – public me and private me and I worried that I had not made greater efforts to keep my baby. The subject was taboo in my family. I did not share my "secret" with friends, became reserved and distanced myself from some former acquaintances.

Although I never spoke to anyone about my baby I never forgot her. Is she making her first holy communion, her confirmation, starting secondary school, how is she doing in her exams and will she go on to third level? I prayed that she would always be good and loyal to her adopive family and that one day she would come looking for me. So my day-dreaming continued for years. I made intermittent enquiries of the adoption agency and eventually got a little information.

As society in Ireland became more open, the subject of adoption was often discussed in the media and stories of search and reunion began to emerge. I read all I could find on the subject and in time, became aware of groups of birth mothers, adoptive parents and adoptees. I went to a birth mothers' group, still suffering from the old prejudices of my generation and discovered that I was not alone. While it was difficult to speak openly after more than 30 years of silence, I realised that all those other birth mothers had suffered similar loss and by sharing our stories, we were able to work through our grief. I did some further research and discovered the name of the adoptive family and where they had lived, and also the date of the Adoption Order. I was overjoyed to see that the name I had given to my baby had been retained and for this I was grateful to her adoptive parents. Following further enquiries at the Agency I was rewarded with a very kind letter from my daughter giving me information about her life, but she did not want contact. I was still unaware of where she was living or what was her married name, but I was happy just to know she was well and happy.

I got on with my life and, in a better frame of mind, another 12 years passed by. Finally a miracle happened. The Agency contacted me with the fantastic news that my daughter was seeking contact. This resulted in exchanges of emails and information about our respective lives, also photographs and telephone conversations. I answered her questions honestly and was deeply touched by her consideration and sensitivity. In fact, it was good for me to deal at last with a difficult part of my life and my hope was that it would also be helpful for her.

Finally, after about two years of communication, we met in person. It was a joyful and relaxed reunion, helped no doubt by our earlier correspondence when we dealt with lots of emotional matters. I know now that my daughter has had a good life, was nurtured within a loving family and is happily married with children of her own. I enjoy very much our regular correspondence and chats and am sure we will continue to be good friends. I am old now, and, having shared my story with a few relatives and friends, am a much more contented person. The long wait for our reunion was worthwhile - my motto is to never give up hope as miracles really happen.

Judy

A LITTLE BOY AND HIS MOTHER

What a glorious sight
yet in me it begins a bitter fight,
a cruel reminder of my own sad plight.

A toy in his hand
the best in the land.
His eyes that gleam and shine
oh God!
how I wish he was mine.

A mother's loving smile
the same one I had for a short while.
My eyes begin to burn
I want to turn and run,
but all I can do is stand and stare
and think how life can be so unfair.

Eight years of pent-up grief
wash over me like a tidal wave,
I think of my little son
and all the love that I gave.

I gave him the gift of life
and myself a mountain of strife.
What should I do with this little bundle of joy,
my precious little baby boy.

Not wanted by anybody but me,
a shame to the family he would be.
My love for him was so deep,
to think of hurting him made me weep.

Your life with me did not bring a guarantee,
so, my little boy I had to set you free.
Give you into the care of strangers,
to protect you from hidden dangers.
Now I finally have to cut the naval string,
and work through all the pain and sorrow that will bring.

Goodbye my beautiful little son.

Rose

A MOTHER'S DAY SPECIAL

They say life is what you make of it, but that adage is not always true. Decisions are sometimes made for you and carry implications that last a lifetime.

It is very difficult and painful to write about a decision that is deeply regrettable. Placing my baby son for adoption 40 years ago left a deep loss and sadness over the intervening years from which I never quite recovered. I had become consumed by the fact that I had to 'find' my son and see him before I arrive at the 'Pearly Gates'. On contacting Cúnamh to help locate him, I had a lot of hope but little expectations. However, it became a very rewarding and fulfilling experience for me. It is true to say it could not have been possible without the social worker assigned to my case. It was through her caring, kindness, empathy and understanding that helped me to make sense of my deep loss and emotional turmoil, that had been suppressed within me for 40 years. It was through our many international phone conversations and emailing that contact was finally made.

It cannot be described the feeling of euphoria, true happiness and joy, it can only be felt that I experienced on seeing my son after 40 years. Our reunion plays over in my mind like a beautiful dream! I was very fortunate that my son embraced me after 40 years and we can look to the future together and not to the past. One year forward, we celebrated our first Mother's Day together, with his wife and my two beautiful grandchildren. Sometimes, I think I have dreamed the dream but the memories are still present.

Julia

ADOPTION

My father died suddenly of a heart attack one week after my pregnancy was confirmed. I stood over his grave at a big public funeral and nobody there knew anything about it. Sometime later my mother was told. She was shocked and was unable to give me any support. I was an only child.

I have been reunited with my daughter for eight years now. Over those years we have built up a good relationship. She is my only child. She is happily married and has two lovely daughters. I am enjoying my granddaughters and also have a good relationship with my son-in-law.

I was thirty-five years old when she was born and she was thirty-five before we had any contact. The trauma of separation from my child persisted from the beginning of my pregnancy up to the birth and after the birth to the time that I gave her up for adoption. All through the subsequent years I grieved and yearned for her and longed to know if she was well, how she was getting on with her adoptive family, and how she was doing at school. I prayed for her.

She was five and a half months old when I gave her up for adoption after soul searching all that time. I believed that adoption was best for her but could not bring myself to give her up. No sooner would I make a decision for adoption than my emotions would change in favour of keeping her. In the end it was mostly others who persuaded me and I agreed to adoption on the basis that she would go straight to her adoptive parents. That was not what happened.

Many years later when we got to know each other better she told me that she was given to a foster mother where she became seriously ill. She was sent to hospital where she was in intensive care fighting for her life. After that she was looked after in a convent for six months. She remembers the nuns and being in a white room. Fortunately she did recover and was given to good and kind adoptive parents.

At the time she was separated from me she was a happy, healthy strong and beautiful child. I never let her see my tears and only let her see the joy she gave me. We were surrounded by people who loved and supported us both.

Her adoptive mother had been seriously ill for a long time and died before we were reunited. Her father gave his blessing to our relationship. Shortly afterwards he died and sadly he and I never met.

I can accept the necessity for adoption but I believe there should be some degree of open adoption depending on circumstances. Every child has a right to know about his or her background and every birth mother has a right to know something about her child. The situation is undoubtedly complex, the adopted child is the child of his or her adoptive mother and is also the child of the birth mother.

My strong feelings are that the mother-child bond cannot be broken and that no legal document can ever break that bond. Nancy Newton Verrier in two books: 'The Primal Wound' and 'Coming Home to Self, Healing the Primal Wound', has extensively researched the trauma of both the adopted child and that of the birth mother. She stresses the primal importance of the mother-child bond and the extreme trauma of the separation for both. I found Nancy Newton Verrier's books helpful in understanding and rebuilding the relationship with my daughter.

I endured the suffering of knowing nothing of my child. From my experience a woman can never forget her child. It is not natural for a woman to be separated from her child for life. Look at nature and watch the lambs in a field. Every lamb knows its own mother. No woman should ever be put in a position where circumstances make it impossible for her to keep her child, or never again to be allowed to see or hear anything about that child and be made to suffer the agony of knowing nothing. It is mental torment for a mother and it is inhuman.

In my heart I never gave her up. There were times when I despaired of ever seeing her again. My husband always reassured me that the time would come when I would be reunited with her.

My sister-in-law has three adopted children, all of whom have annual meetings with their birth mothers. Both she and her husband can accept and cope with that situation. Recently we had a beautiful family gathering with my daughter, her husband, and her two children, my sister-in-law, her husband and their three children and my husband. It was a wonderful and happy occasion.

Being reunited with her has brought a huge change in my life. It is hard work, but it has brought fulfilment that I never would have dreamed of.

Alma.

EXULTANT

Exultant, Exalted
Miraculous Moment
Birth!
Alive
Me alive
He Alive
Never Me no More
He and Me forever More!

Fades
Faces of Fear
Sear!
Failure
Forget!
Forget..Never!

Promise
Me to He
Promise!
I will be back!
Don't forget me!
I am returning!

No Nun
No sham
No shame
Will stop me!
On my life
On my Breath
On my Spirit!
I will be back!

Walk the long
Walk!
The Corridor!
Hand Over!
Over!
Never!

Despite
their Spite
we reunite!
Reunion!
Rejoice!

Time was stolen
but a moment
is a lifetime!
The force of
Mother Love
Could tumble
Rome!

Time to move!
Time to Forgive
Pity the ones
who tried!
Fake false
fools caught
in their
own gauze.

Mother Love
Eternal!
Mother love.

MHR

HAPPY BIRTHDAY CÚNAMH

The heartache of walking away from St Patrick's Home on the Navan Road, Dublin and leaving behind my beautiful baby girl would be the hardest thing I ever had to do in my life. And then to think that I would not set eyes on her for another 34 years.

But I promised her that I would find her. And I did.

A million thanks go to the wonderful social workers in Cúnamh who gave me such good advice and support and as a result I am in constant contact with my birth daughter and our friendship is going from strength to strength. I was especially privileged when she came to my home for a visit in the summer of 2011. It was a magic time.

I am looking forward to the future and at last I can say that my heart is healed.

Geraldine

I WAS TRULY BROKENHEARTED

To be honest I knew very early on in the pregnancy I would give him up for adoption. I don't recall any other choice available to me. I mean if I wanted to go to college and carve a future for myself there were no supports available to me if I had kept him. I felt he would grow up in poverty and without a dad.

Before he was born I stayed in Eglington House, which was actually quite a pleasant place. I had the honour of meeting the late Garret Fitzgerard a few years ago – and I mentioned I stayed there. He told me I stayed in his mother-in-law's room.

When my son was born that is when the decision really hit me and my journey began. I was truly brokenhearted. I couldn't even visit him in the hospital. I was, I think, a broken person. My next big memory is signing the papers – you know at the Home it was easier to give a child up for adoption than buy a house (even in the boom!).

My main focus was to give him a stable and secure life. No matter how low I got that's what I focused on. I was lucky in a way in that his adoptive parents were open about the adoption and over the years I got lovely letters and photos. These kept me sane and kept me going during my lowest points.

Was it the right thing to do? Who knows, I mean things did get better for single mums so maybe I could have done it! The reality is he had a great childhood, he did everything I could have wished for. He never had to worry about anything really, knowing that makes anything I went through worthwhile.

I have learned two things over the years as a result of giving him up:

There is no point in longing for something you cannot have – it will eat you up! The reality is a parent would suffer anything for their child.

Niambh

LIVING WITH A SECRET

When I fell pregnant forty-three years ago I had to keep it secret from everyone including my siblings. My mam and dad were the only ones who knew. They sent me away to have the baby adopted, I didn't have a say in the matter.

When my daughter was born I had to look after her for six weeks before I had to hand her over to her adoptive parents, that was the worst day of my life.

After I handed my daughter over I had to return home and carry on as normal, which was very hard.

Thirty years later I was in a position to tell my siblings, they were shocked but at the same time very supportive. I endeavoured with enquiries to find my adopted daughter's whereabouts and to find out if she was happy. It has taken some time, but we have met and I know now that she has found happiness and love with her adoptive family, and I am equally happy for her.

The adoption agency was most helpful and offered me guidance and encouragement. They organised the meeting and they provided us all with backup and reassurance.

Breda

MY ADOPTION STORY

The saddest day of my life was when I held and kissed my beautiful five-day-old son for the last time before I left Holles Street Hospital in 1978. I was not in a position to keep him then, and I felt adoption was the only way to go. The years seemed to fly by so quickly. But not one day ended without me thinking and longing to know how my son was. It felt like a constant ache in my heart.

Throughout the years I kept in touch with the social workers in Cúnamh and found I could talk to them about my son. I always made it known that I would wish to meet my son, if and when he ever wanted too. So with the wonderful help and support from my social worker, we started to look for him. After a couple of years searching he was found. With my social worker's help my son agreed to me emailing him. We got to know each other over the next few years. We spoke about the time of his adoption, and his parents, who gave him such a wonderful upbringing. Not once did he judge or hold any resentment towards me.

Last August 32 years after that sad day in 1978, my son, David, asked to meet me. I had the great privilege to once more feel my arms around him. No words can ever express how I felt. My heart just burst with love. Not only that, but my son is now a father himself. My grandson is now 8 months old and it's just so joyful to have them in my life.

Ruth

MY HEART ISN'T BROKEN ANY MORE

To help explain my story, I first of all would like to give a brief background to my childhood as in my opinion this leads on to the situation I found myself in as a 17-year- old.

From the age of two I was placed through the Irish courts into an Institution that was known then as an orphanage until I was 16. Without going into too much detail I had the most awful upbringing imaginable. Then the Order decided to move me on at 16 and in their wisdom got me a job as a servant with a Doctor's family.

With no knowledge of the outside world and totally institutionalised I surely was a lost soul.

Within a short time I met this boy called Paddy who showed a lot of interest in me. I was swayed by his attention and also fooled because of my naivety and ignorance. I fell for his charms. So in no time at all I became pregnant. Looking back at that time I had no one to turn to. No family, no support, no birth cert, no knowledge of any kind as to who I was.

I remember as a child being tormented by the local town's people when we went for Sunday walks in groups. We used to stand out a mile, we were so badly dressed, always cold. The names we were called were so cruel. "Here come the orphans". Writing this down is still bringing tears to my eyes.

So here I was pregnant, learning as I went along, at this stage I had to accept that Paddy had lost interest and abandoned me completely. The agony of it all was hard to bear. What could I do?

I knew where Paddy lived. I decided the only thing I could do was turn to Paddy's family. So building up some courage I found myself at their door not knowing how they would react. After the shock of it all they turned out to be wonderful people and in a way took control of the situation.

Paddy lived with his aunt who had a sister living in England, so they decided the best option was to go there. From the start Paddy's aunt and her husband did all they could. A lot of the everyday stuff is now a blur. They were such sad times for me and yet without their help God knows where I would have ended up.

I went along with the family's advice, that was to have the baby and then adoption. I never saw Paddy ever again, in a way we were both immature kids at the time.

Paddy's family got in touch with (Cúnamh) a Catholic Child Care Agency who arranged for me to go to a Mother and Baby Home in Ireland with the intention of adoption in due course. I went on to have a beautiful healthy baby boy whom I called Philip. I had him with me for 6 wonderful weeks. The torment of it all was hard to bear.

Here I was in a state of depression having to return to England. Yet again Paddy's family was willing to let me stay with them. I shall always be grateful to them. To this day we are still good friends.

As time went on I had to get on with life and deal with the trauma of it all. I got myself a job. It was then I met John. We hit it off and fell in love. Marriage soon followed and then three children. Although I settled down to married life and all my energies went into rearing three well adjusted lovely children Philip was never far from my thoughts.

Just to finish with a bit of good news from my part. My heart isn't broken any more. With the help of Cúnamh I was able to meet Philip for the first time after 47 years or so last year. We are now in regular contact and making up for lost time. I am heading for Dublin soon to meet the rest of his family.

Imelda

My story begins in 1971

My story begins in 1971. I was a 14 year-old teenager full of fun, giggly and silly: Jackie Magazine provided me and my friends with fashion and make-up advice, topics of conversation, personal advice and pin-up posters of our favourite pop stars. I had girlfriends and I went out with boys. Having a boyfriend is the culmination of joy for every teenage girl although, in my mind, I knew I was going to marry David Cassidy the pop singer. Then, that summer, I met a special boy. I was madly in love with him. My new boyfriend was 3 years older than me: a tall, elegant, pretty boy, he became my friend, my passion, my world. I transferred all my emotional fervor to him. We walked, talked, danced and played the days away. I thought this wonderful existence would last forever.

We were together a year. I was growing up fast but at 15, three years is a lot of catching up to do. Soon, without knowing it, I was in over my head and I was pregnant. It was May 1972. By October I was not well and my parents took me to a doctor and the news was out. My 16th birthday was in November. It was a lonely, empty one. It should have been a sweet time.

I left school (a convent) in October, under the pretence that I was going to study in a private college. That sorted that out. My father was furious. My boyfriend's mum was a widow. There were family meetings. There were ugly scenes. I was the apple of my parents' eye. An only daughter among sons. One was outraged - he was the wild one! The eldest, who was married, was sympathetic and tried to calm the situation. Only one was younger than I. We were very close. I thank God for that. It was hard to tell him and explain what had happened. It meant he had to grow up too but he was to keep me sane the next few months. He was in school with my boyfriend, who by now was doing his Leaving Cert. My brother kept a line of information open between us, delivering letters and notes.

My parents did not know this. They confined me to the house. No one was to know. If family came to visit I was banished upstairs. I could only go out for a walk at night-time so no one would meet me. My mum didn't know what to think. My father blamed her. She let me go out with boys. He was scathing about her part in the whole affair. Bad feeling grew like a dark cloud over our home. I know mum had plans to keep her first grandchild, (I noticed that she was putting away baby clothes), but she was afraid of my dad. He was very upset. I was clever and he had high hopes for me. It was to be a miserable Christmas, the saddest I can remember. I felt so alone, sitting with the Christmas tree whilst everyone went to parties and left me on my own. Then I would catch a few moments and I talked to my boyfriend on the phone. I tried not to give in to tears, I did not want my baby to experience unhappiness before she was born. There would be time for tears later.

Some nights I met HIM quietly on my walk. I was afraid to use his name now. It was cold. We just stared at the stars and just held each other not really knowing what to do or what would happen to us. I remember those nights so well. I didn't want to go home. I even contemplated killing myself. My father had threatened to accuse him of rape, as I was under the age of consent when I fell pregnant. It was too horrible to think about. His future would be ruined. He was a good guy. We were only guilty of loving each other.

I was a small girl, there wasn't much of a "bump". My romantic nature kept me going. In my isolation I played my music, painted, wrote poetry and dreamed of being a mum. I kept my studies going too. Oh, I had no doubt that my mum would keep my child and we would all live happily ever after. I thought we were part of the new age. Wrong again.

The visits to the social worker at The Irish Catholic Protection & Rescue Society started. An old, foreboding building with endless climbing stairs and dark rooms. My mum came with me for all the visits but I only remember one, the interview with the priest. I didn't like the questions about my personal life. I don't remember my mum being there, but she was, always. I don't even remember the social worker at all. I knew they were going to take my baby. I didn't want to be there: I did not want to be a part of this. I was not married and my parents were becoming ashamed of me, I thought. Looking back now 39 years, they were protecting me from a backward nation, stigma and conventionality. They did not want me exposed or hurt. Wrong again. This hurt never goes away.

My daughter was born on St Valentine's Day. I told you I was a romantic. My doctor had to bring me to the hospital as my father was away on business. I remember little of the birth. I never saw my child. She was taken away. The next morning I looked out the window, snow had fallen, it was a winter wonderland. My father came in smiling and told me I had a little girl. I felt sad for us. He loved little girls. His attitude had changed but his mind was made up. My mum never saw her granddaughter. I don't know if that was my father's doing. But my mum was never the same again. She got depressed and ill. It took years for her to get through it. I carried a lot of guilt after that. The "secret" had become too much for mum and me.

I gave my baby a Gaelic name. A name that would have a meaning, a name we would never forget. We never have.

I went back to school 3 weeks after the birth. It was like it had never happened. No one noticed. No one knew. One of my friend's little sister was pregnant. The nuns were doing everything they could to help her through school as she was keeping her baby! I was happy for her. In 1974 I graduated from secondary education with honours.

The doctors thought there might be a problem with my daughter's health. She went into foster care until given a clean bill of health. I prayed she would not pass so we could take her home. She did pass and she was taken into the adoption system at 3-months old and given to her new parents.

My brother arranged for me to meet her in St. Patrick's for a few minutes or an hour. I don't remember. But I am grateful that he did. I have at least the memory and pleasure of holding my lovely little girl for that one time. She was beautiful. I felt blessed.

I signed the final adoption papers in May 1973. I made the journey alone to the solicitors. No one knew I was going. And no one asked. I was 16. A big decision for one so young. So final. I did not want my child's new parents to be worried that I would come looking for her in a few years. I wanted her to have the best start in life. The best family. Security. Happiness.

Eileen

SOON I WILL MEET MY SON

Soon I will meet my son; it's been 39 years since I last saw him. At 17 I was a carefree young girl who met a nice guy who was about 8 years older than me. I became pregnant to this guy and much as I liked him I knew he was not for life. I did not tell him about being pregnant but I have a feeling he knew.

I grew up in rural Ireland, oldest of a large family who did not have much money; we were typical of Irish families at that time. My parents knew about my pregnancy and as much as they wanted to help they were not able to, in those days shame in the family was a big factor. After a lot of discussion it was decided my baby would be given up for adoption to have a better life. I went to an Unmarried Mother's Home in Dublin which was run by nuns who looked after us all (other pregnant girls).

When my son was born I told myself that I would not be parted from him no matter what, but a few weeks of reality check, like where would I live, how would I support him etc, with a heavy heart I gave in and let him go to a better life. Handing him over to the Social Worker was the hardest thing I ever had to do as I knew I would not see him again, after a lot of tears he was gone.

I wandered around aimless for a couple of years. Travelling helped ease the pain, so I decided to emigrate which was the best decision for me at that time. Along the way I met a man who was also adopted and we got along great together and became soulmates. We have made a life together, we did not have any children, it wasn't meant to be, but he has 3 lovely girls from a previous marriage and we all get on great together and have a special relationship, and I treat them like my own. Life moved on and gradually the pain of loss became less so that I could remember my son with a smile and not sadness.

Some 38 years later I got a text message from my sister saying she wanted to speak to me about something very personal and I knew in my heart and soul that it could only be my son. She read the letter to me that came from Cúnamh and shock set in, it took a few days for me to summon the courage to call Cúnamh as I had no idea what to expect. The Social Worker was wonderful and soothing and helped calm me for a while as my inner thoughts were going haywire.

Just knowing a little about my son was enough to send me to an emotional meltdown. I couldn't believe what I had done. Why did I do it, what was I thinking, so many questions. For a few days I was unable to get out of bed. I just lay there in both physical and mental anguish my mind went over everything that happened in my life over and over again. Once again I had to get a grip of myself and thought about meeting my son. We have distance between us so letters are how we are communicating. We have now exchanged photos so I have an idea of what he looks like and he me. Neither of us knows where it will go but hopefully we can be friends that's what I will be aiming for. It has been a long hard year wanting to know so much but I now have to be patient.

Without the help and support of my social worker at Cúnamh and some family members I don't know how I would have come through this, as I never expected to see my son again. It will be 39 years.

Mary

SUPPORT THROUGHOUT A PAINFUL PERIOD IN MY LIFE

I am so grateful to Cúnamh for their support throughout a painful period in my life and throughout the years also.

From the word go they were a listening ear at the end of the phone when I discovered I was pregnant, single and scared. They provided practical help and support and were very supportive through the process of adoption. As a devastated, guilt-ridden, full of shame and heartbroken mother I was determined that if ever my baby wanted to contact me, I would make finding me as easy as possible and to make sure that there would be no doubt about my response of love should this happen.

Years later I kept in contact with Cúnamh and an amazing, professional and warm relationship with the social worker at the end of the phone progressed. She was supportive, wise and very loving and funny. By the Grace of God I was contacted and subsequently met my grown-up adult child and I am eternally grateful for such a miracle. Not everyone has such an outcome. Cúnamh provided a haven of warmth and privacy for us to meet and talk as it is such a private matter and the experience was incredibly special and beautiful. I will never forget that day and cherish it in my heart forever. The connection I made with the Cúnamh social worker was very special as she was such a key in the process and I just thank God for her sensitivity and wisdom. The timing was perfect and I am still amazed at how wonderful things have turned out. I am writing this to bring hope to you if you are someone in my position and to convey how heart wrenching and painful it is, to someone who may have been adopted.

Geraldine

THANK YOU

It was November 1983. My girlfriend, after 18 hours of labour, gave birth to the most beautiful baby girl. I held her in my arms for a while, counted her toes, and noticed that her second and third toes were webbed like my own. It was a very emotional day for us, and one that I will never forget.

We had decided over the last few months to name her Catherine. We had also made the decision to give her up for adoption. We chose this course of action after many weeks of back and forth. In the end, we thought that Catherine would have the best chance for a good life with parents that had a career, and the economic means to take care of her. The adoption agency had been very helpful and had promised that they would find a good home for our baby.

As a young couple who had given up their first-born, we were unlikely to stay together. She was such a loss for both of us, that everything else was meaningless. I left for the USA in 1985 without finishing my college degree, and tried to never look back, but I lived with this guilt and loss on a daily basis. I can only speak for myself, but I know in my heart that it affected Catherine's birth mother deeply too.

In 1998 I was diagnosed with leukaemia. The doctors gave me a twenty percent chance to survive five years. I received a stem-cell transplant from my sister, Sandra, who was a six for six match. It was a long road to recovery, but I was glad to take it.

It was many years later, in July 2008, that I received an email at my work from my daughter's birth mother. She had registered on the National Adoption Registry a few years earlier. She let me know that she had been in contact with the Adoption Agency, and had actually written and received letters from Jenny (Catherine). She asked me if I wanted to get in touch with the agency. I told her that I would be delighted.

She had given me the best gift that I could have ever received. She told me that Jenny was doing well, and had grown up in a happy home with wonderful parents and a great younger brother. I wrote to the agency social worker and with her help and guidance, I wrote my letter to Jenny. A few weeks later I received a lovely letter from Jenny that filled my heart with joy. She told me all about her childhood, her parents, her brother, and her passion for sports and reading books. I found out that she was fluent in Spanish, and had lived in Spain for almost a year. She had also been to Argentina, where over half my family still live.

The first time I spoke to Jenny on the phone, we spoke for an hour and a half. I guess we had a lot of "catching up" to do. It was wonderful and very special. We also spoke in Spanish and I was impressed with her Andalusian accent.

We met for the first time in Orlando, Florida. She was there on vacation with a couple of good friends. We were both nervous but we got along great. She invited me to go to Disneyland the next day with her friends and we had a great time. Jenny has since been to our home several times. She was here for Thanksgiving and has met my wife's side of the family. My wife, Michelle, could not have been more supportive from the start, and I will always be grateful to her for this.

I want to personally thank Jenny's parents and brother for being so open and welcoming to me. Without their support, my new relationship with Jenny would have been very difficult, or impossible. They were so kind and warm when I met them all in their home in Dublin.

Jenny came over to us this September for two weeks. Her brother also spent a weekend with us at the same time. We had a great time showing both of them around the beach cities. Her parents flew in to spend some time with us. We all got together several times for some great meals and a boat ride. I will always consider them family.

I have lived with my loss of a child since I was twenty-one, and I have been quite hard on myself for over twenty-five years. Since reuniting with her I have been comforted in the knowledge that she grew up in the right home, and she has turned out to be a lovely person, on the inside as well as the outside. I feel that the world is a warmer, more inviting place, that some things happen for a reason.

Thank you Cúnamh for all the good you do.
Thank you Michelle for your never-ending support and love.
Thank you to Jenny's birth mother for tracking me down and making sure I got in contact with her.
Thank you Jenny's parents and brother for being such a great family to her.
Thank you God for not taking me away when I had leukaemia.
Thank you Jenny for being such a wonderful person. You were always in my heart.

Trevor

THAT SEPTEMBER DAY

On that day, I knew, I just knew. A soft voice spoke to me, I knew. "I am getting my baby back." This powerful feeling immediately came flooding into every cell of my body.

This was emerging for me after the twenty-two years of my baby's precious life had been lived. I am getting my baby back. It is time now, maybe next week, to be with my daughter again. Everything will be well. All I could see was my baby and me. In the following days, I had a sense that I was apart from the world and everyone in it, I was present and yet I wasn't present in this world. Almost as if my body had naturally sedated itself, and I was being carried, mind, body and spirit.

I continue to be a bundle of calm, excitement, anxiety, fear, calm, disbelief, excitement. But my intelligence has some understanding of the complex time I have ahead of me. Inner peace flows through me, in the knowledge that my beautiful daughter wants to reconnect with me. I am blessed. I brought this precious young woman into being. Now, I feel completeness as a Mother. Now, I feel completeness as a woman.

It is now, reconnecting with my daughter, I will visit all in my life that brought me to where I was, and where I am. "Whatever happened in your life, between the said years, is the raison d'être of your existence," he said this to me. He did not know, he could not know. These words reinforced for me the torturous joy and beauty life is. This is for me; this is ordained for me, from the beginning of time. It is a certainty; my daughter had to be born.

The "hush hush" was there for me. "Will they hear about you in the town?" she said to me. When I described to my Mum, how beautiful my pregnancy and delivery was, she responded nearly dismissively, "you will have more children," was she feeling her loss too. For a fleeting moment, I thought she is coming to mind me and my baby, to take us home. She came to see us, she held my sweet baby in her arms. All too much, she wasn't there. Never would my Mum speak of my baby and me again. I have a great sadness that my Dad never knew. He would have loved my gentle baby girl.

Over my lifetime, the hurt that this pressurised decision has created for me; and the worry and fear of what it could have done to my precious child, has been with me since her birth. My sweet baby, I kissed your perfect, healthy, beautiful, gentle body all over. My chest swells with love and pride for my beautiful baby, child, woman. This is falling in love. I have fallen in love with my baby. Proudly, I am walking, my hand in her hand. I feel our smiling eyes sweetly lost in each other, our beings sinking into each other when I will hug my baby again.

Hours of talk are pulling out my great strength, for now, and for the road ahead throughout our reunion. A great strength I always had, I didn't know this and now I do. I didn't know how to get to know myself. I know now, and the knowing continues. How will this strength be called on. When will this strength be called on. How and when my girl needs and wants me, I will be a safe and secure holding place for my daughter.

My sweet, sweet little girl baby, I let you go on your way. I have never let go of you. My little spirit of this world, you are coming back. Did you take a piece of me with you, is this bringing you back to me. Have we a connection that will go on.

Her words to me are love. Her sweet and gentle and hopeful words in my hands can't shake my fear. This powerful fright has every cell in disarray now, from sedation into disarray.

Now I am living in the fear that I will lose my daughter again. All powerfully present for the moment. Never in my life did I examine Faith. At times now, feeling lifted up and carried, when I must surrender to Faith. I must trust now. Faith and trust will guide me now. Where Divine timing and will are my protector. This way, I am ready.

Two years have passed now since that September day. I can wait, I will wait, to kiss my gentle baby again.

Lily

THE JOY OF REUNION

My son was born on 9th April 1968 and six weeks later I relinquished him for adoption. I simply had no choice. But nothing quite prepares you for the absolute anguish and despair of handing over your own flesh and blood whom you have carried for nine months, given birth to, and love with all your heart. It was the worst day of my life and the pain and heartache of that day will remain with me forever.

A few months later I moved to London to start a new life. In time, I met my husband and we returned to Ireland and got married in 1973. In 1985, with two children under our wing, we emigrated to Australia.

Unbeknownst to me, my son had begun his search for me prior to me leaving for Australia so when he got news that I now lived in Australia the search came to a stop. However, many years later, he took up the search again and this time I received a letter from Cúnamh. To say I was completely thrown would be an understatement. I had no idea how I was going to handle this reunion emotionally as I was unable to even talk about what had happened thirty-eight years previously, the pain was so deeply buried. My husband had always known about my son but my children had not been told. I felt I needed to tell them first but this too was proving emotionally very difficult. I knew my son was waiting for a response and would be hurting but I seemed powerless to move. I would 'talk' to him daily in my head telling him I would not let him down the second time, that I was trying to get there. It may seem difficult for anyone who has not lost a child to adoption to understand my behaviour at this time but when you have had a severe trauma in your life that event can disable you emotionally and you need professional help in order to progress. One day I arrived home from work sobbing, as I did most days thinking of my son, and fell into my husband's arms telling him that I needed to get some help. That night, with his help, I wrote to Cúnamh. It was October 2005 and the start of my journey.

As soon as I received my son's first letter in reply to my own, just in time for Christmas that year (talk about Christmas presents!), I sat down with my children to tell them about their brother. They received the news with absolute delight and in fact they opened a bottle of champagne to celebrate having a new brother. For almost a year my son and I wrote to each other and exchanged photos, it was always a red letter day when the postman delivered his letters. They would be next passed to my husband and children, all eager to read his news. I was also having one-on-one counselling, as well as telephone counselling from Cúnamh, which was very painful but necessary. The day I could talk about my son without sobbing was the day I knew I was on the mend.

Our first phone call was scheduled by Cúnamh for 5th August 2006, a Saturday night, I was to call my son at an agreed time. All day I fretted and stressed, this was huge for me, I was finally going to speak to my son. Then I dialled his number and as soon as we spoke it was as if we had always known each other, it was so natural, we just laughed and chatted with such ease. Both of us had taken a box of tissues to the phone in case they were needed, but there wasn't a moment's pause on either side as we excitedly chatted away, both having to fight to get a word in as we had so much to say. I will never forget the happiness I felt after that phone call, you could not wipe the smile off my face!

Our reunion was set for 11am on Fri 8th September 2006 at Cúnamh so I flew in to Dublin the previous afternoon having left Australia with the love and best wishes of my entire family and close friends. I couldn't wait now for the moment, I was itchy with excitement. And then it was time. I will always remember the moment when my son walked in the door and we both put our arms around each other, it was sheer joy. I didn't ever want to release him. We had come full circle and my happiness was now complete, I had my beloved son back in my life. We saw as much of each other as we could that first week and every moment spent together was so special. The pair of us just clicked instantly and we are so similar in many ways, the same sense of humour, both love to talk and sometimes we would even go to say the same thing, it is uncanny. The genes are definitely there!

My son came out to visit us in Australia the following January and we had a great welcoming party for him. He has been back on three occasions since, the last visit for his sister's wedding in November 2010. His sister and brother have both travelled to Dublin at different times to spend time with their brother as the three of them get on so well. I try to visit at least once a year as I now also have two beautiful granddaughters whom I love and cherish. Of course I do wish the distance between us wasn't so great but we try to make the best of it with regular phone calls.

My journey of reunion has been one of great joy and happiness. Thank you my precious son.

Dee

THE NEW MOTHERS' SMOKING PARTY

Bathrobes, slippers, swollen bellies and bloodshot eyes,
clicking, flickering cigarette lighters
the smell of smoke stings my eyes,
the men's sweaty palms,
toe tapping agitation, cravings for fast food, the dark fortress of
the old Coombe casting a shadow on our smoking party
the women's labour stories and stitches
their surrender to nature leaving them loose limbed and
bedraggled
yet victorious and glowing
and
who am I amongst these women?
What right have I to a place amongst them and why do they
intuitively accept me?
I, like a ghost, returned looking for my lost forlorn past.

Anonymous

WHEN I FOUND MYSELF PREGNANT

Yes, mother and baby together is the best option.

Unfortunately this is not always possible.

When I found myself pregnant, and my family found out, things went from bad to worse. It came to the stage that I could no longer stay in the family home.

With no place to go, sick and feeling I had no one, only my unborn baby to love, a work colleague gave me the contact details of Cúnamh or CPRSI as it was then. I didn't know anything about them.

After a "rough" spell, my sister and her husband brought me to their home in Dublin. This got me away from the rest of the family where no one would know me. My love grew as my unborn baby grew. I had intense feelings for my baby. I wanted hope and a future for my baby. Over time I decided to go and see what CPRSI had to offer.

The day I arrived at the big Georgian House I was frightened. As I rang the bell I wanted to run. Immediately, I was greeted by a very friendly person. Nervously, after telling her I had an appointment, she showed me to the waiting room. I heard slow steps coming down from above. The squeaking door opened and a person spoke. As we went up the steep narrow, creaking steps, I was terrified. We went into a small room, with a table and 3 chairs. When she began to talk, I immediately started to feel my body relax. She told me a little about herself and the place. She invited me to tell my story. I felt so at ease. She explained to me, I was doing a great thing for my baby, looking at the different options. She was happy to help and support me all the way.

As they were an adoption agency she told me what was needed to be known. I remember her saying she knew great couples that would love my baby, give it a secure future. After a few meetings with, as I now called her, "my social worker" I began to consider adoption. She asked me to write down the advantages of keeping my baby and the disadvantages, also advantages and disadvantages of adoption.

With the situation I was in at the time the adoption option was getting stronger and stronger all the time. With my pregnancy coming near an end, I asked my social worker to help me with the adoption road.

As luck would have it I went 12 days over my due date. I loved each day, as I had this time with my baby, so much so that when I finally went to the hospital, I just got there on time to have her safely delivered.

As I looked and cuddled my new baby, I promised her that I would do my best for her. She was beautiful (perfect) and deserved a fair chance in life. This was difficult for me, as I didn't know where I was going. On the third day I phoned my social worker and told her my baby was born, and I'd like her to come and see me. I felt at peace when she came in as we both talked about my daughter and the future. I felt at ease to ask and sign papers to proceed with placing my baby in foster care.

There was intense pain, but, as I saw my child would have a loving secure family, I did not want to let her down.

She went into foster care, and with the support of Cúnamh (CPRSI) I signed to allow her to go for adoption. I wanted her to be with her parents as early as possible so they could enjoy her, and with as little effect on her as possible.

Cúnamh contacted me with details of parents for my child. Cúnamh invited me to meet with them. This meeting is very blurred in my memory as it was also the final day I would hold my baby. Nevertheless, I can still see the couple who are the proud parents of my daughter, her mum sat emotional, holding the very first picture I had taken of, now, "our" daughter. Her dad asked as many questions as possible so that he could tell his daughter as she would ask.

As with all good things Cúnamh kept us in touch. All I ever had to do was make a phone call and they were ready to support. Whether it was for myself or enquiring about my daughter, they were always very helpful.

Now 24 years have passed and my grown-up daughter has been in touch with Cúnamh. This progressed to Cúnamh contacting me and inviting me to write to her. We both have the same social worker so it's great to talk to her as she knows us both. With a lot of support, my daughter and I are on the journey to getting to know each other. As you can imagine after 24 years we have a lot to write about. The letters and photos are toing and froing from Cúnamh with ease.

At present we are building a good foundation to ensure a lasting monument.

It is an amazing journey, love, heartache, and pride. None of it would have been possible without my daughter, her adoptive parents and no way least Cúnamh.

Ann

SONG FOR MY SON

Where are you now, my baby?
Are you living close to me?
What are you thinking now, my sweetheart?
And what is your philosophy?
Has life been good to you, my darling
And do you know I hope and pray
That if you ever have the time, babe,
Please come and look me up...Someday.

So many questions now to ask you,
Like where you've been and what's your name?
And though we know I had my reasons,
Every one of them seems lame.
And how I hope that you'll ....Forgive me,
And do you know I hope and pray
That if you ever find the time, babe,
You'll come and look me up....Someday.

And do you look like my father
Or his older brother John?
Or do you look like my mother or her mother's only son?
A reflection of my own son, the one I never gave away
And if you ever find the time, son,
Please come and look me up, Someday.

And if you ever find the time, son,
Please come and look me up.

Reproduced with the kind permission of the author Mia Parsons from the CD "Oceans and Other Short Stories"

AN OPEN LETTER TO MY SON

It is not without a tinge of regret at times that I realise what I have missed, celebrating birthdays and Christmas together, reading you stories or going to the park. There were times that I cried for you and times when I was sad. This sadness could be overwhelming and debilitating. I won't go into too much detail, but there were moments when I could not go on, or felt I could not. However I have survived and today I am happy to say that I am in the final year of my degree of a B.A. in Humanities.

I have come a long way from the naïve young woman I was back in 1985. It can be quite a feat to recall everything that happened twenty years ago, but what I do remember vividly is your birth. You were tiny, a lot paler than I imagined you would be and very beautiful and very healthy. I held you, I fed you and I cuddled you. I loved you with all my heart. For the few days we spent together in the hospital, I cherished you. It was the last time I would see you. For I knew I could not keep you. This may seem very hurtful and a little harsh, but it could not be otherwise.

A week later I left the hospital, empty-handed. It has been the hardest most difficult thing I have ever had to do, the worst decision I have ever had to make. Believe me it's true. You, my darling son, remained in the hospital. I could not visit you or be with you, I was grounded. Your grandfather would not allow it. Please be assured, it was a different time. I received word nine months later that you were in foster-care, at least I think it was nine months. I have to be honest and say I cannot be sure, as it is a long time ago. Then the whole adoption process was in motion. It didn't seem too long after that I was signing the adoption papers. One thing I can recall though was how supportive the adoption agency was, I do recall visiting the social worker, and if I remember rightly, I did receive counselling. I could not bring myself to think about it too much. If I did...well it did not bear thinking about. I knew I did not have a choice. Please remember it was a different time...and please don't ever forget, you have always been in my thoughts, you have been with me every step of the way.

Fast forward again another few years, over time I had received photos of you as a baby and of your tender years. I loved your curly hair and your wonderful smile, you looked happy. On your birthday each year I would cry, at Christmas I would feel down. I wondered deep down with each year passing, how you were, what you were doing, how you were getting on at school. What your new family were like. Fast forward once more, maybe five years later, your mum has contacted me. She has written me a letter to keep me up to date. I won't go into too much detail lest I embarrass you. I know how it is when your parents embarrass, although they don't mean to...most of the time. Ahem.

I must add that all through this process of searching for you, then hearing from your mum and receiving the latest photos of you, the social workers and counsellors at Cúnamh have been so supportive. Every step of the way, they have counselled me and supported me. They have been honest and direct and I really appreciate the help they have given me throughout this difficult time. They recommended a course and a focus group, I did go to some of the nights, but found it heartbreaking and too raw to open up. It was though a very valuable experience. It also made me feel I was not completely alone in my experience and that there were other birth mothers out there who felt the same and had gone through the same thing. All those years of waiting, wondering and finally meeting our lost children. All those years of support and encouragement from Cúnamh social workers and other staff, past and present, have not been forgotten. It has taken a long time for us to meet and finally we did. An eventful day to say the least...what more can I say. There is nothing more I can say. I was speechless when I saw you. You are so tall. Where did that come from? I am short and stumpy and well everything's going south for the winter, I am in my autumn years, the wrong side of forty, fast approaching fifty!

I must take a break now. I will write again soon. Hope to see you again soon. Take very good care of yourself. With love,

Sandra

Our Journey

My darling daughter,

It seems a life time ago since our journey began. And yet it could also be only yesterday, your birth and the pain of parting. Everyday I wish things could have been different and, everyday I hope to be reunited with you. I know you have made a great success of your life. You have excelled at your studies, got married, and now have two beautiful children. I couldn't be more proud of you, and hope you can forgive me for giving you up, believe me, if there had been any other way.... Although I wasn't there for your forward journey through life, I never stopped thinking of you, loving you, and wishing only good things for you and yours.

Your loving mother x

ADOPTIVE PARENTS SHARE THEIR STORIES

WHY I ADOPTED

My reasons for adopting a child were, to some extent, selfish. I can make little claim to piety, and I did not decide to adopt a child merely because it is a good and charitable thing to do. I adopted a child because my wife and myself wanted a child.

We had married young – at least we were young by the standards of rural Ireland – and like all young people we faced the future with an abundance of hope, and with little else. The death of our own child did little to diminish that hope, and we thought that it would be only a matter of time until we had others. We had names picked out for them.

But they didn't come. The years slipped by, and we slowly came to realise that we were a childless couple. We had acquired many interests to take up our spare time, and we had a vague sort of notion that, some day, some one of our nephews or nieces would come to live with us.

They didn't come either. Even a favourite godchild couldn't be spared by a mother, though she had the full of the house of children. We drifted along up to the 40 mark, and when I passed it I began to feel the first cool draft of an oncoming loneliness. The prospect of a lonely old age is not a bright one.

I know what loneliness is. As a youngster I had worked in a strange place where the people had no use for those whose accents betrayed them as mine did. In two years there I didn't get to know a dozen people, and I hadn't a friend to turn to if I had needed one.

Neither did I want to drift into a crabbed old age. Loneliness is bad enough, but it is infinitely worse to be so governed by moodiness that you become a nuisance to yourself and to everybody around you.

The only way to brighten the prospect seemed to be the adoption of a child. We called at the office of the Catholic Protection & Rescue Society, and from the very first moment we had complete faith in the officers of that Society.

They agreed to give us a child. We didn't mind whether it was a boy or a girl or even twins, as we hoped to adopt more than one. They gave us a boy.

And what a boy! There may be boys just as fine in the country, but I doubt it. Certainly neither my wife nor I would admit that a finer child could possibly exist.

He was a year-old the other day. He weighs 35 lbs. He has three teeth, his legs are like young oaks, and there is strength and power in every inch of him. He is big, and – like all small men – I admire size.

His coming changed our whole outlook on life. We had been inclined to settle ourselves securely in our narrow little grove, but he yanked us out of it. He opened up for us a fuller life which we are enjoying to the full.

Our neighbours, a conservative rural people, might be expected to be suspicious of such an innovation as the adoption of a child. They were not. They came, bringing presents, to welcome that baby with a welcome that was as sincere as if he had been born to ourselves.

It may sound ridiculous, but my wife dreams about that child every night. I dream about him every day. I can see him throwing the hammer to victory in the Olympic games of 1980. I can see him at some outpost of Africa spreading that Faith which is the priceless heritage of the Irish child.

That child has brought a new light into a mother's eye, and a new determination into a father's heart. Nothing else could do it, for not even Wagner could create as glorious a sound as the laughter of a happy child, in a childless house.

Timothy
Written in 1960

A Forensic Adoption

There I was on my knees, not that I am an overly religious person. In fact it had nothing to do with prayer, although I had been praying over a long period of time. No, on this occasion I was on my knees putting dust on a door in South Anne Street.

I had been sent there earlier by my boss to examine the scene of a burglary over the weekend.

I had introduced myself as a detective from Pearse Street Garda Station at the premises and was now doing the mundane usual job of examining the scene.

So there I am on my knees on South Anne Street. with my brush and dust when I hear a voice above me say,
"What in the name of God are you doing?"
I looked up and met the gaze of a middle-aged lady looking down at me with a puzzled look on her face. Although she wasn't smiling her face was very friendly. She was trying to get into the building past me at this stage.
"I am trying to find fingerprints; I am a detective from Pearse Street."
"Oh, we haven't had another break-in," she replied with some annoyance.
"Afraid so, it's Monday morning in the City Centre and the burglars have been busy as usual over the weekend".
"And are you going to catch them this time?"

I had often heard that question before and I gave the usual answer.
"If I find a print here then the culprit might as well have left his name and address", which wasn't always strictly true, but it sounded reassuring to the poor victim. The lady then said "do you mind if I watch what you are doing, it looks very interesting?" "Please feel free but it is not very exciting," so she stood and watched as I did the job.

I then said the words that changed the lives of my wife and myself forever.

"What is this place, the C.P.R.S.I.?"
The lady said "this is the Catholic Protection and Rescue Society of Ireland." "And what does that mean?" I asked, wondering what Catholics needed rescuing from. The lady said that they helped with families in trouble and with children and they also provided for adoptions.

At the word adoption I stopped what I was doing and without looking up I said "I am tired of that word, adoption." "Oh and why is that?" I stood up and looked straight at the lady and told her that for the past number of years myself and my wife had visited every adoption agency in the country and we were turned down by them, all for one reason or another and that we had given up on all hope.

At this stage I was sorry that I had asked what they did in the building as it had brought up the hurt of it all. The lady never said a word, she just stared at me as if she was trying to read my mind.
She then said "my name is .... come up and see me when you are finished."

Now this was a normal request for me on Monday mornings at the scene of crimes. It usually meant that you were going to get a telling off from the irate victim of the latest crime. I understood this and was well used to it.

When I was finished I went to ......office for my scolding. I knocked on the door of her office and was beckoned in "now", she said, "sit down and tell me about yourself and your wife." I said "what has my wife got to do with this?" "Well, you were telling me about the trouble you had in relation to adoption." I didn't know what to say. I was thinking "is this woman going to help?" I said "we have been disappointed so often please be careful what you say." "I want to know all about yourself and your wife, I won't make you any promises but bring your wife in and we will talk."

I ran out of the place and went straight home without going back to work. I couldn't ring my wife as we had no phone and depended on a neighbour's phone but it was too private to be ringing them and this all happened before the era of the mobile phone.

Anyway I told her of my meeting with ...... and we started to have meetings with her and 9 months later my neighbour gave me a message to ring ...... (we still didn't have a phone), I walked to a phone box and phoned her. When I did, she said "we have a baby girl for adoption, do you want to come and see me?" I actually started to cry on the phone as I said, "yes we do."

We now have a grown-up daughter and son, who are the light of our lives and we are so proud of them.

Over the years, Cúnamh, as they are now known, has been a real home to us as the children have grown and they still talk about the visits they had to Cúnamh every Christmas to say hello to the wonderful people there.

I have often thought of the times we knelt to pray for a child without an answer but it was while I was on my knees on South Anne Street doing my job that God did send an Angel with his answer.

And so ends this story.

Gerard

ADOPTION IS HOW WE BECAME A FAMILY

Why their eyes are brown and mine are blue
How he's so good at football and I haven't a clue
Why she's got golden streaks in her stunning red hair
And why we use words like 'birth mother' in our evening
prayer.
Our family wasn't made in the traditional sense of things
And we embrace the differences, and all the challenges that it
brings

I love the sound of their little feet running down the hall,
It's half six in the morning and now he wants to play ball.
We enjoy the usual highs and lows that every parent knows
Squabbling, demanding and keeping you on your toes.
There are sleepless nights, time-outs and toilet training
Baking cookies, adventures and boredom when it's raining
Our children may not have grown in my tummy
But make no mistake I am their mummy

With little to go on, we have no idea of how our children will
grow
Like a blank canvas, with no expectations, as no one can
know
To us they are like stars with talents that will shine bright
Just need a little encouragement and an opportunity to get it
right.
Whatever you inherit from a family we know little about
We will always be there for you to guide and help out.

Adoption is how we became a family.

Dee

EMOTIONAL AND HUMBLE

The week prior to our son Joseph coming to live with us was like a roller-coaster. It was the happiest, exciting, scariest and most exhilarating time for my husband and I. The phone call came on a Monday morning and we met our social worker that afternoon, where we were told all about Joseph. My stomach was doing somersaults all day. The next day we met Joseph's birthmother and her mother, two lovely people, and through a lot of tears we heard all about our son. After that meeting we knew everything was going ahead.

We met Joseph for the first time in his foster home. His foster mother is a special lady who had looked after Joseph for almost five months. He was such a happy, contented child who loved his food and has a lovely little laugh. We fed him, held him and laughed with him.

A couple of months later, Joseph's birth mother and her mother came to visit. We had a lovely visit. We see them at least four times a year every year and we have a very great relationship with them. I like to think of us all as one big family. We are very lucky.

Two years later I gave birth to a little sister for Joseph. This completed our family. When I gave birth to our daughter, my thoughts went to Joseph's birth mother and her time giving birth to Joseph. It made me feel very emotional and humble (it still does!).

Joseph is now 12, loves playing Gaelic football, hurling, basketball, golf and karate. He likes school just like most 12-year-old boys do!

Life is good and I cannot imagine it without Joseph or his sister.

Carole

COMING OUT OF THE SHADOWS

I am a Mum through adoption, was blessed with the gift of a baby boy to have as my own . . . . but never just my own, always in the shadows was his birthmother. His first smile, his first tooth, all the innumerable firsts of every child I celebrated but she hovered close in my thoughts and in my heart. What was she doing? Did she suffer an enduring loss in the decision she made? I prayed, *'Please be okay, birth mother of my son, I want you to be okay because the gift you bestowed on me made me okay'.*

The years passed, he grew up. We talked about the shadow lady, his birth mother. *'Yes, you should search'*, I advised, *'how wonderful it would be for you and for her'*, believing the rightness of this sincerely and wholeheartedly. No, he chose to keep her in the haze, which I respected . . . . with relief!

He became a man, not always so sensible but always so loved! One day a call came.....to me! *'There has been an enquiry.'* What! This shadow lady dared step out of the shade! Instant primal, heart-wrenching pain! *'He is mine! Oh gosh, is she okay? What does she want?'* Tears, sobs. *'Is she okay? I am so glad!.... Tell me! Don't tell me! Don't give her substance, don't make her real!'*

My son was told. Though saying little but knowing him so well his almost imperceptible nod said it all. Yes, this is so right but why is something so right so painful, the pain of 'right' so acute and so wounding?

Time passed. Letters and photographs came. *'Oh, she is lovely, so young! How was it for you, birth mother of my son? . . . . . Go away, leave us alone! You made a choice! . . . . but how was it for you, birth mother of my son?'*

They met, embracing him going to meet this shadow lady I wondered how different he would be and how different he and I would be on his return. Yes, it is so right but so hard!

Slowly my son and his birth mother found their way, sometimes just as two and at other times with family, both ours and hers, the ease between these two people a consistent confirmation that this should be so. As they moved forward, reconnecting, I bore witness to what is so right, each being brave enough to find the other made each of them more whole, more complete.

'Oh, birth mother of my son, you bestowed a precious gift to me and my gift, no, not my gift but my duty, to you, and to my son in return, was to hide my pain, my initial jealousy, yes, my jealousy, and to support wholly and lovingly this relationship in its infancy until cemented and forged.'

'So birth mother of my son, in those early days I wished you had remained in the shadows until one day, when you asked, " How is your son?," I could truly respond calmly and with certainty, " he is not my son but ours." Then and only then did I finally allow you to come into the light, out of the shadows, never to return.

A number of years have now passed since that call came, my adopted son and his birth mother now have a close, gentle relationship which will only continue to strengthen. My biggest fear was losing him but, no, I'm still his Mum. Instead of loss there has only been gain. Two people, who, in different circumstances, should never have been parted, are now in each other's lives. As for me.....my life has also being enhanced, not only by seeing my son blossom, but by the warm friendship that has grown between my son's birthmother and I.

'Thank you, birthmother of my son for having had the courage to take that risk,' from your son's adoptive mother.

Sheila

FROM 6 TO 7

We were a family of six,
2 boys and 2 girls, a mam, and a dad,
We decided to share our love with someone less fortunate and
sad.

We got in touch with Cúnamh to ask about a baby.
They said they'd do some checks and then, well, maybe.

We got a call to say we'd gotten our first little boy.
For seven wonderful weeks he filled our home with joy.
Then the day came when he had to leave,
We were all so heartbroken, lord did we grieve.

Babies have come and gone,
We've loved each and every one but one pulled at our hearts
and we just couldn't part with Kevin.
Now we are a family of seven.

Charlotte

ADOPTION MADE OUR FAMILY

Adoption made our family.
Adoption changed us from wife to mam and husband to dad.
Adoption is how our children will grow up our children.
Adoption is how my daughter became my angel
And my son became my prince.
Adoption is how they have a brother and sister.
Adoption fills our house with love and laughter
Adoption changed our world for the better
Adoption helps us live our dream
We are a family because of adoption.

Dee

LOOKING BACK

You know when one day you are sitting at home and something happens to bring your mind back to past events or your outstanding memories, well such a thing happened to me about two months ago when I opened a letter from Cúnamh and read about their proposed book and asking if we, as parents of adopted children, would like to contribute to the book with our experiences. Well my mind immediately went into flash-back, recalling all that had led to our applying for adoption and all our experiences. I suppose it must begin back in 1981 and our wedding day, we were so excited, happy and scared, our whole adult life ahead of us together, then getting on a plane for the first time going on our honeymoon, everything was perfect. Then in 1982 we bought our first house, we were scared, we had a mortgage (although a car costs more today) and yet we were so excited we really were on top of the world and nothing was going to stop us. We sat by our open fire in the sitting room of our home making plans for the house and our future. We would do up the house room by room and agreed we would not start a family for two to three years. We were young, in love and had it all in front of us.

Well the two or three years flew by and the house was coming along nicely and our thoughts turned to the family that we so wanted and were ready for. So we decided the time was right for us to start our family, we had reached another new milestone in our lives and everything was still perfect. Another two years went by and we were not pregnant, we did not panic but both of us could see that the other was slightly concerned but did not want to raise the dreaded subject. Eventually we talked and agreed that while it was probably nothing maybe we should talk to our GP. Of course she agreed that it was probably nothing but to be sure she sent us to the hospital fertility clinic. So began the next chapter of our lives and this chapter was a lot more stressful for both of us.

Then one day two years and many tests later my wife said "that's it", enough tests, we need results and we made an appointment and faced the doctor like two schoolchildren. That day we thought our world had ended and our hearts broke when he said "I'm afraid you won't be having a family naturally as there was indeed a problem". We were shattered, he explained that there were other possibilities but we could not hear him, all we could think was that this could not be possible. We drove home that day and never spoke a word to one another, but we both knew in our hearts we had to face up to this. We had to go through that mourning period (for that was what it was). Then one day we had a good cry together and agreed we still had one another and we would accept God's will. Our talk eventually turned to our options as we really wanted children and we discussed adoption.

And then it happened we received a letter from the CPRSI asking us to come for an interview, we could not believe it, we went through so many emotions, happy, scared, delighted, fear.

We got notice of our first home visit, we both took the day before off work, we cleaned the house top to bottom (twice), we discussed what we should wear, should we make tea, maybe sandwiches, biscuits, cake, we should not appear too anxious, but eager enough at the same time, god were we nervous. We did that visit and many more over the next two years, and answered questions about ourselves and each other and our views on life and after every visit prayed, worried, re-examined every answer we had given hoping they were the right ones.

My office phone rang, my wife was screaming down the line, I could not understand her, was she hurt, was someone dead, no, we were getting a baby, she had the letter. I drove to her mother's house tears in my eyes and she ran out to meet me, we stood there hugging, kissing and crying. I read the letter we have a baby girl for you, could we collect her on the following Tuesday. We only had eight days, we had nothing, no clothes, no cot, no pram, no room ready, no nappies, no baby food, our minds were in a spin. I took the rest of the week off, we shopped till we dropped, we could hardly bear the wait.

Then the day came and up we went with our Moses basket, we were brought into a large room, big fireplace, the door opened and in came our social worker and a foster mother with our beautiful daughter, she handed her over to us. "The world was perfect," we were parents, we were a family.

Our daughter is nineteen now and our son is fifteen and the joy, love, happiness and sleepless nights they have brought to us cannot be expressed in words. My wife and I still consider ourselves the luckiest people in the world.

Andy

LAURA

Until today you had no name,
"Laura"
What a pretty name.
I never gave you a name,
all through the years.

Until today you had no form,
"Petite"
Well not too tall, dark hair
And....Your eyes...Blue.
She said you were pretty.

With every descriptive word,
I took a step backwards,
With every descriptive word,
You took a step forward.
I've been centre stage for so long,
While you remained backstage.

Husband on the phone said,
Don't worry we've done our job.
I didn't want it to be a job,
A career is what I craved.

MOTHER TO MOTHER

Nobody ever told me how deeply I would come to love you both over the years of loving our children. Nobody ever told me how my heart would strain to embrace you at birthdays, at Christmas and on special days or any day.

I have never been alone all these years. You are the ones I turn to in recognition when surprised by our children's unexpected gifts. You are my close companions in the joys and challenges of mothering – in our children's struggles and achievements. I am your companion always in your pain of separation.

Nobody ever told me how deeply your hope would become my hope. I pray that one day soon our hopes will be realised. We just have to trust, as mothers do, that our children will choose what is best for them, not simply for us.

To the mothers who gave birth to our two adopted children.

D

SOME MOTHERS

Some mothers can't look after babies because they are unwell or for other reasons. But they want what is best for their baby.

Phyllis

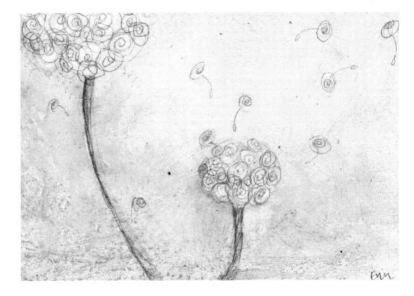

Those four clever, talented, articulate people

Beginning with the most difficult thing about the total experience of adoption - it was when we first had to draw up the subject between ourselves. All attempts at achieving a pregnancy had failed. We had spent five years trying – had done all the tests – adoption had to be mentioned. We each knew our own individual attitude to adoption but what if the other was not open to the idea. Phew! What a relief when the brief discussion was over. No reservations on either side.

Ahead full steam. Appointments with Social Workers – nervous at first but generally looked forward to each one. We felt the process was moving us closer to holding our baby.

Apparently, in the course of these meetings, we were asked if we would be willing to meet the birth mother. Though neither of us recalls being asked, apparently, we were enthusiastic.

The call came, along with a request that we have a meeting with the baby's mother. We discovered later that this was far from routine procedure in Ireland at the time. It was a measure of the professionalism of the Social Workers involved that we had no idea that they were sweating more than we were. Later, when things had gone well, they let us in on the secret.

At the beginning of one of those long hot summers of the 1980's we arrived home with our bundle of sheer joy and I remember that year as being the most contented time of our lives. Of course there was the steep learning curve that parenting brings. However, those sunny days are etched in the memory as if frame by frame.

At this point a very early question, asked by a dear friend, comes to mind – when are ye going to tell "x" he's adopted?

I remember my answer, which came swiftly and without hesitation, "I hope we will never have to tell him because he will always know". We always felt we knew his mother and similarly with his brother three years later because we also met. It was easy to say "I think your mam was also left handed – or your mam loved travel – was athletic – loved chocolate etc". Frankly I think the poor lads probably got a surfeit of it! I have always felt at one with their mothers. I assumed that we would meet again.

We had a blissful "childhood" – as parents I mean – it remains for the boys to assess how pleasant or otherwise they found the experience. The teens brought the expected anxieties. The usual stresses were there but adoption brings extra baggage. We were assisted in understanding this by our oldest lad. He is a born communicator and explained the "burden" that it creates. He articulates the rejection well.

Almost thirty years has passed – not everything turning out the way I foresaw it. The journey towards reunion has been bumpy. I've learned that it's their journey – the two mothers and the two young men. We have had a wonderful experience over the three decades – influenced lots of decisions – now it's probably time to take a back seat and let whatever happens happen. Those four clever, talented, articulate people – four people I love in different ways – will work out how things should be.

Norrie

OUR ADOPTION STORY

When my husband and I were asked to write about our experiences, thoughts and feelings on the whole adoption process we were not unduly perturbed. After all we had devoted the last eighteen years of our lives to it from the very first letter of enquiry that we wrote to an adoption agency to adopting our son 15 years ago and our daughter 12 years ago, right up to the present day. We were not prepared in any way shape or form for the huge swell of emotion that arose while revisiting the very early dark days when we discovered highs and lows. We had put to the back of our minds all of the huge insecurities that we had as we longed to be chosen as adoptive parents, the seemingly endless wait and our panic and fears as we met the birth mothers of our children.

Our lives are totally fulfilled now as we raise our two wonderful children, the answers to all of our prayers, dreams and hopes. They fill our every waking moment with joy and happiness. We don't remind ourselves daily that they are adopted even though it is a very important fact in all of our lives. Instead we are like any other family getting on with our busy lives.

Our experience of adoption has been a most positive, wonderful life-altering and totally fulfilling one. We feel that as people we have grown and developed in character as a direct result of our experience and regard our infertility now as having been a blessing in disguise.

Before we learned that we were an infertile couple we were like any other young married couple in the world. We had hopes, plans and dreams of having a family together. As time went by and nothing happened we become a little concerned but didn't worry unduly about it as we reassured ourselves that "these things happen" and we just needed to be patient.

Time passed by and our worry became quite real and tangible. We began to ask ourselves what we would do if we could not conceive. Doctors often delay investigations so we had plenty of time on our hands to discuss and to worry about this possibility. The one thing that was constant in our conversations was that having a family was the single most important thing in our lives and that we would leave no stone unturned in our quest to do so. It matters not whether it happens early into your infertility investigation or later, the decision to stop putting your faith in the doctors and medical procedures and accepting your diagnosis is an enormously difficult one. It puts a final full stop on your dream of giving birth to a child "of your own."

There was a time of mourning after this for us as a couple. We were devastated. We felt lost and at sea. Our dreams of having a family seemed at that point in our lives would remain forever such "a dream." We kept the knowledge of our infertility to ourselves. It was to become a very private grief. We accepted the doctor's diagnosis quickly but learning to live with it was difficult. There were days when we were very positive about it and were able to say to each other that if we were to remain childless we had plenty of love in our marriage and that would be enough for both of us. Then there were the heartbreaking days when we would remember that having a family was a most important aspect of our love.

We knew that the route to adopting a child was a difficult one. We knew that this would not be an easy journey but nothing had been easy for us so far so we were very strong and determined about the whole process and were ready to commit ourselves totally to it.

We attended the first meeting full of trepidation and anxiety. We were afraid that we might say something wrong and fail before we had even begun. Our abiding memory from that meeting is the feeling of hopelessness when it was over as our very wise and experienced social worker had left us under no illusions as to the difficulties of the road we were about to take and the slim chances of success. Our hearts were extremely heavy as we returned home that day.

We had not reached this point in our lives by lying down under the weight of worries so we pressed on. Having had much medical examination and questions about intimate areas of our lives in the past we did not have difficulty with the many personal questions that were asked during our assessment process. Sometimes after a meeting we would analyse the answers we had given and worry. We would think of what we should have said or ways in which we could have said things better. When our assessment was finally over and we were told that we had been successful in getting our names on the waiting list, words cannot describe how happy we were. This was the first bit of positive news that we had been given since we had begun trying to start a family. It was the first time we had been given hope.

Yet there were many times during the next two and a half years when we felt like giving up hope. We kept constant contact with the agency and it with us. The agency told us that there were very few babies being placed for adoption. Our primary assessment had to be reviewed and updated every six months. Meanwhile we were getting older and were very conscious that a young girl might think us too old to become the parents of her baby.

The days that we found out about our son and later our daughter are forever etched in our minds. We can remember every minute detail of them, the exact time of the day, what we did and most of all the sheer joy that we felt. Both of our children's birth mothers requested a meeting prior to their final decision to place their children with us for adoption.

We were extremely nervous before both meetings. We knew that both mothers had accepted us as parents on paper and we were terrified that we would not live up to their expectations, that in some way they would be disappointed with us. We were very conscious of the age difference between us and them and worried that they might think us too old. (We were aged 33 and 38 adopting our first child).

If we were feeling so nervous and insecure we were also very conscious of how both birth mothers must have been feeling as they made this enormous life-altering decision. We never under-estimated how difficult it must have been for both very young girls to face such a meeting. We expected the meeting to be extremely emotional for all of us.

What exactly was said at the meetings and how long they took are a blur now after all of the years but we will never forget both very positive experiences. Today we have a very clear mental picture of both birth mothers as a result of these meetings. They both made a lasting impression on us, one that we can share with our children. When our children ask us questions about their birth mothers we have a very clear image of them in our minds when we answer.

In the beginning our written correspondence with the girls was quite factual. This was a result of initial nervousness we felt on our side. We were very conscious of the hurt and loss that the girls were feeling and we did not want to be insensitive by writing "too much", by perhaps "gushing with our joy" and maybe in turn hurting or offending them.

As the years have passed we have all relaxed totally with this very successful arrangement we have with both birth parents. We write our letters from our hearts, as they should be written because we feel that this is the only way we can write truthfully about our children to their birth parents. Then they can get a true sense of what their birth children are like as they blossom and grow. We feel that if and when our children search for their parents and finally meet them, their birth parents will know much about their children, making truly getting to know each other much easier.

We work hard to lay solid and very positive acceptance of the fact that our children are adopted with them. We, in fact, celebrate it. We, as parents, hope that with the open communication we have with the birth parents of our children, when we finally meet up, the reunion will be a successful one for all. The children will be fully aware of what has been happening in the lives of their birth parents and so there will be no surprises or shocks in store. Through the steady communication that we have with each other their birth parents know what their children look like, what they like and dislike and their different personalities. Our children's birth parents are part of our lives today. We look forward to the day that we will meet the girls again and hope that in the future they will always continue to be part of ours and our children's lives.

It is not often that someone can say that the worst thing that ever happened to them in their lives became the best thing but we say this from the bottom of our hearts. Being diagnosed as infertile has resulted in the enormous blessing of two wonderful children by adoption. Truly we have been blessed.

Paula

FROM AN ADOPTIVE MUM TO A BIRTH MUM

I can still see the sorrow in your face.
As you opened your arms and we embraced.
This little girl, so deep in your heart.
The pain of giving her up tore you apart.

We know your heart is broken in two.
But she will always be a part of you.
Everytime she smiles up at me
It's her birth mum's face that I can see.

And though she's not in front of your eyes.
She is there with you in your everyday life.
I'd love to comfort and hold you as you cry,
But do not be sad, it is not goodbye.

You may not be here to hold her tight.
Or tuck her into bed each night.
But your precious angel knows who you are.
Although the miles between us are far.

We are both her mum don't you see.
She is a part of you and a part of me.
So let go of the pain and bury it deep.
A lifetime of love is yours to keep.

Be strong, we love you so very much. Thank you for sharing
your beautiful daughter with us. We think of you all the time.
You are a part of our family always and forever.

Cathy

ADOPTION THOUGHTS

Impact of Infertility

Nothing could have prepared me for the long empty road that infertility took me through - it was similar to the effects of an anesthesia, numbness and an inability to move your train of thought or body on little else. It was the results of a laparoscopy that was to finalise everything - my days of wandering through long hospital corridors and crowded waiting rooms were finally over in the endocrine clinic. My dreams of a future with a large family lay shattered and despair, bitterness, anger and sadness were just a few feelings to mention. Endometriosis was the clinical reason for this and it was a severe case of it that treatment undertaken was not successful.

Somehow very slowly I managed to deal with this and accepted it but only time allowed this to happen - it certainly didn't happen overnight. It was only at this point of acceptance that I began to look at other options reminding myself not to have any high expectations - I learned that lesson already and it is said you can only break your heart once so it was not going to happen again.

We had so much to give to a child and we were determined to do our best to fulfill the dream of parenthood.

Sandra

Confirmation of acceptance to undergo an adoption assessment

We waited patiently and after a short period we got confirmation for an assessment - this was a day I can honestly say I smiled from my heart all day. It was made very clear that there were no promises or guarantees and it enabled us to take this very slowly and not to have those high expectations that lead to shattering disappointments and grief.

I will be forever thankful to our fantastic social worker as she saw me laugh and subsequently cry - her work was carried out with complete professionalism, compassion and kindness whilst at the same time the priority lay constantly with the interest of the child. This assessment, if I'm honest, was very tough and it was one of the most challenging and self-rewarding things I have ever done and I am forever thankful for the manner in which it was carried out.

Sandra

Receiving the letter of acceptance

The immense joy that this letter brought us was unimaginable. We did not care that we could be waiting a long time, just to know we were well on our journey to becoming a family.

Maria & Harry

Hearing the news

I sat there with tears flowing down my face, but laughing at the same time. That phone call and memory are etched permanently in my brain, and can still bring tears at the thought. There were two people close by with very worried expressions on their faces. When I explained the phone call, they started crying too. I worked in a large company and word spread like wildfire. I tried ringing my husband but was crying so much, that he thought somebody had died. I eventually managed to tell him, and he was as shocked as me. Never in our wildest dreams did we think we would get a baby so close to Christmas. The worst part was that we had to wait all weekend as we had to meet the birth parents on Monday.

Karen

The news arrived to us that would change our lives forever. We were to become a Mammy and Daddy. A baby girl. We could not have been happier than we were that day. The excitement throughout our home, our family and friends was unbelievable.

We had our meeting with our daughter's birth mother. The joy and the sadness of this day will always be kept by both of us.

Maria

Meeting the birth mother/parents
We had only four days to prepare for his arrival, and during this we had our meeting in Cúnamh with his birth mother. As with our meeting with our daughter's birth mother, this day is forever in our hearts, the same feelings of sadness and complete happiness mixed together. Both of these meetings were and still are of the most important and best things we have ever done. We also had to prepare our daughter for her new baby brother. We have a lovely photo of her taken on the day, her last day as an only child.

Maria

It was the hardest weekend we have ever put in. I don't think we slept at all. By Monday the nerves had got the better of me, and I started panicking! What if the birth parents don't like us? I remember sitting up in the waiting room in Cúnamh and looking down at the old rug and thinking "well at least if I get sick, they won't notice". The meeting went well, except for the first five minutes, where I was struck dumb with nerves. They were as nervous as us, but in the end our social worker said they loved us.

Karen

I was lucky enough to meet my daughter's birth mother. It was such a happy time for me yet such a heart-breaking and devastating time for her. I instantly felt such a connection with her when we hugged - that moment for me was so emotional when I assured her that her little girl would always be loved unconditionally by both of us.

Sandra

Meeting the baby

I was feeling so, so nervous and apprehensive. What would he be like? We hadn't seen a photo. How would he react to us? OMG I knew nothing about children! Panic – what would these foster parents think of us. With sweaty palms and shaking with anxiety, we rang the front door bell. The foster father, with a big booming Yorkshire accent, opened the door and welcomed us in. Go right in, he said. We rounded the corner and there was the foster mother, with Josh on her knee. She had him turned around to face us. She must have given him a little tickle because just as our eyes saw him for the first time he had a big, broad smile and such a happy, laughing face. He was, without a doubt, the most handsome baby I had ever seen. Oh, he is gorgeous, we repeated. Our eyes couldn't leave our baby. Was he really ours? Could we really be that blessed? Would this work out? He came to us no problem, without making strange.

The foster mother asked if we would like to feed him his lunch. Panic all over again – would I be able to without making him cry, without making a mess, without looking like a total amateur. Half an hour later and pureed carrots mainly confined to his face, hands and the bib – ok there was some, just a little, on his t-shirt too and I thought this is going to be okay.

Two engineering degrees is no match for the five-point harness system of a baby car seat and we had to resort to reading the manual to get him strapped in!

What an exciting, thrilling, surreal few days....all the excitement and thrill of meeting a baby was repeated a mere fifteen months later when we met our second son Mark.

Paula & Padraig

How we got through the next week, I will never know. It was like a rollercoaster of emotions and in the space of one week, I knew our life was about to completely change. I actually lost half a stone in that week, and all my friends laughed that while everyone else piles on the weight with a new baby, I was losing weight. I hadn't a clue what to buy but all my friends came to the rescue. Friday finally came and we were exhausted and expecting something to go wrong all week. What if they change their minds? However, we were handed our baby boy just after 10 o'clock on Friday the 20th December and it is true when they say it was love at first sight. He was only 8 weeks old with big blue eyes and was dressed in white from head to toe. There were tears all around as the foster parents said their goodbyes. Half an hour later, we were walking up Grafton Street with our new bundle of joy. We were both so nervous but elated at the same time. It was surreal. There was only 5 days to go to Christmas and we had this beautiful baby. I really feel he was heaven sent. It had been a long struggle with many disappointments along the way, but the wait was finally worth it. As I write this the baby will soon be 15 years of age and we now have the teenage strops, but I would not change it for the world.

Karen

Our day arrived and I know that we both did not sleep the night before. We made our way to Cúnamh and we knew the route so well but today this journey was so special, today we would finally become a family, this day we would remember forever.

We arrived to Cúnamh and we went in to the Waiting Room, this room we knew so well. We were called in and we had a chat and finally our daughter was brought in to us. I asked for her, to be placed in her Daddy's arms, I could not take my eyes off her she was just so beautiful and perfect. When she was placed in my husband's arms she just looked up at him and smiled. I knew then we were a family.

We travelled home but on the way we went to the Phoenix Park. This was a place that held great memories for me as this is where we went as children on Sundays with my mam and dad. This was where families went to and we were now a family. We asked a passer-by would he take a photo of the three of us. We arrived home to a tremendous welcome from family and friends. Everybody was so happy for us that our dream had finally come true.

I finished up work and we began the journey to the baby shops. These you must know are places we never went to because they made me so sad, and now I could not be taken away from them. We made our purchases, a new three-in-one pram, mamas and papas baby car seat and baby monitors. A little note on this, as adoptive parents we only had one week to prepare for our baby not nine months so all my nesting for my baby was done in that week.

Maria

Thoughts on birth mothers

A day never goes by and especially on Mother's Day that I think about both of their birth mothers. This day is so special for me and I am sure for them it brings sadness. If one good thing is to come from my story is that out of sadness brings so much happiness. Always remember you are both always only a thought away from us. Thank you both.

"Our children were placed into our lives but they were born into our hearts"

Maria & Harry

OUR THREE ADOPTED CHILDREN

Dear Michael, Helen and Shane,

It would indeed be impossible to sum up in a few short paragraphs our journey as parents to you, our three adopted children, whose lives we have been blessed to share during a period that spans more than three decades. Filled with hope and fear, with dreams and tears, we anxiously awaited news from Cúnamh, the agency in which we placed our hope and trust. We knew for certain you would light up our lives. During the year-long waiting period, you grew within our hearts as we waited to love all three of you. Carried on the wings of destiny, you Michael, the oldest of our three children followed by Helen and Shane, were placed with us. You brought us immense joy and happiness, a wonderful sense of purpose, fulfilment and gratitude and at times, feelings tinged with sadness, knowing for certain that someone somewhere was missing each of you, who no doubt continued to be your guiding stars.

The following short poem titled The Gift of Life might help describe our feelings towards each of you.

The Gift of Life
"I didn't give you the gift of life,
But in my heart I know,
The love I feel is deep and real
As if it had been so,

For us to have each other,
Is like a dream come true!
No I didn't give you the gift of life,
Life gave me the gift of you"

Author Unknown

The enormous love we felt the moment we saw you was only the beginning of a deeper and richer love that would steadily grow in our hearts, binding us together for all time, making the present possible and enabling us to dream of and imagine the future. Your arrival in our home heralded lots of changes, new routines and no routines, well-made plans that mostly became unstuck. Our lives at times seemed topsy turvey, our home became a noisy place filled with your gurgling sounds, your cooing and shouts of laughter. We loved and cherished magic moments, like feeling the velvety touch of your skin, seeing your soft sweet smile, the first tooth, feeling the grip of a tiny finger, hearing your first words, along with countless milestones, that marked the ordinary and uneventful days of each passing season, giving us lots to talk about, lots of memories and numerous stories to tell our family and friends. The once-tidy, organised rooms were now strewn with baby's things, with bottles, colourful toys, books, high chairs and an endless supply of washing, ready to be put on or taken off the clothes line. But this only confirmed our happiness, delight and new sense of purpose.

Soon we observed your determined spirit as in no time, the sounds were to be heard of knees and hands brushing against the floor, scurrying in and out of rooms, crawling to greet a visitor at the front door, numerous attempts at standing and falling and trying all over again, fascinated and inspired us and even made us laugh.

We saw with our own eyes your strong, independent spirit and quiet confidence, slowly but surely blossom as we soon witnessed the miracle of the first steps cautiously taken, in great excitement and pride, bringing us admiration, joy and relief.

Life became even busier as further milestones were reached. Starting school in your brand new uniforms, making lots of new friends, wanting to show us your new found independence by walking into and out of the school on your own, talking about teacher and the events of the day, doing your homework etc were reminders to us that time was indeed marching on and as the birthday candles were blown out each year, and we all sang Happy Birthday, we knew for sure you were growing up.

Communion and Confirmation days were memorable events for many reasons, not least because we knew you were now not only an integral part of our family but also of our local community and of our parish. We were truly proud when we saw you looking splendid – a million dollars, calmly and confidently taking your place in the Church with your class-mates and friends and afterwards at home during the celebrations with grandparents, cousins, extended family members, neighbours and friends.

We feared for you as the big move to Secondary school loomed ahead. How would you cope with so many new faces, so many new subjects, a huge building, a long day? No amount of reassuring on your part would allay our fears and anxieties for you. But we hadn't taken into account your independence, ambition and growing maturity and like so many occasions that were to follow, you responded to the challenges with a steadfast and unwavering determination, displaying your own talents and abilities, while confidently crossing each hurdle. Your hopes and dreams, fears and frustrations we shared, daring to expect and maybe even believe that somehow things would fall into place for you. We wanted everything good life could offer you and wished only for the best, hoping that fate would be kind and generous to you.

We have truly learned that though we may wish, we cannot halt the march of time. All three of you have "flown the nest", and are leading your own busy lives, facing daily challenges, following your own dreams and daring to live them. Our love for each of you remains constant and unwavering. Now we find ourselves telling you our worries and cares, always valuing and appreciating your support, goodness, opinions and advice given in the spirit of friendship. You have walked the journey of life with us, sharing its joys and sorrows, highs and lows, trials and tribulations, enjoying the sunny and bright times together while supporting each other during the darkness.

The cycle of life continues. The birth of our beautiful grandchildren has filled us with awe and wonder as well as deep gratitude and just like you did, they too light up our lives. They are a constant source of joy and happiness to us and suffice to say we adore our new role and status.

We have been very blessed by the goodness and kindness of a number of people whose paths we crossed during a very important time in our lives, without whose help and intervention we could not have managed. We mention our social workers in Cúnamh whose unwavering support, advice and guidance helped and sustained us through the process and long afterwards. Mile Buíochas.

Finally, may each of you continue to follow your dreams and may happiness, peace and joy surround you now and always.

With much love

Mam and Dad

OUR TWO SPECIAL BOYS

We came together as two but wanted to share our love as a family

Alas we learned that this could not be

We could only dream of you but never thought it could be real

But then you came along and our hearts filled with joy

Our joy became pride as we watched you grow

Then one became two and our circle became complete

Every day we watch you play and talk and share

Although sometimes we act sternly it is only love that we feel for you

You are our two little miracles and everything we feel is for you

You can be everything and anything that you want to be

But remember we will always love you and cherish you for the gift that is you

Our two special Boys!

David & Eileen

Out of the darkness and into the light

Have you ever had your worst nightmare come true? Well I did.

From as early as I can remember being a "mother" was the most important thing in the world to me. I was never career-minded or ambitious in the workplace because nothing else was more important than giving birth, being a mother, rearing a family and always being home for my children as my mother was for me.

We were two years married when out of the blue I was diagnosed with "ovarian cancer", which led to a complete hysterectomy to save my life. We were completely heartbroken and utterly devastated. How would our world start turning again?

Then utterly by chance, we heard about Cúnamh. We applied, were accepted and underwent an assessment and to our unending joy were lucky enough to adopt two beautiful baby boys. How we loved them from that first moment we saw them. Then and only then through Cúnamh did I get the chance to be a "mother". Finally, I was complete and I couldn't love them more if I gave birth to them myself.

Cúnamh made our world turn again. They became our friends and they understand so well what adoptive parents go through as well as the wonderful, brave women, who for one reason or another, have to part with their children. Through their support and friendship Cúnamh are always helping couples like us to create loving families.

Paula

RECLAIM

Do I tell you about the two fantastic children we were so blessed to have adopted from Cúnamh and who make each morning such a joy to wake up too. They are our world and what we always dreamed of and we love them both unconditionally, but the story I feel I must tell is that of our first adoption that ended so sadly in a reclaim.

It was amazing, we couldn't believe it had actually happened to us! We are standing in a room in Cúnamh looking at the most beautiful little boy we had ever seen, he was just perfect, absolutely gorgeous. We took him in our arms and from that moment on he was spoilt rotten and we didn't care, he was such a joy, a real bubbly child. Life was great, full of plans and great expectations for the future. As regards the paperwork of the adoption I suppose things did seem to be moving slowly but we were not too concerned as we knew these things take time. I was aware that it had been many years since a reclaim had last happened but in our minds that wasn't going to happen to us... or so we thought.

Fast forward nine months to our son's first birthday and we are in the same room in Cúnamh this time handing our son back. About two weeks before his birthmother decided she wanted him back, we couldn't believe it. Two weeks of sheer hell is the only way I can describe it, trying to snatch at any kind of hope that we could keep him. We tried solicitors but as we suspected we had little rights as adoptive parents as no final papers were signed on the adoption. Then we had a little hope when the birthmother decided she might go for open adoption.

This was great, we would do anything to keep our little bundle of joy. He was everything to us and we could not bear to lose him. It was agreed that we would meet and his birthmother came to our house with some of her family. The agenda was to discuss terms for open adoption. We had our social worker there and after his birth mother had spent some time with our son (and hers) we sat around the table to talk. It was strained and we were extremely anxious and nervous. Things didn't go according to plan and his birthmother decided she was going to take him back...the shock was unreal. I really cannot describe the horrible feeling at that moment, it's like someone punched you with so much force that you felt you would never get up again.

I remember I got a nose bleed which would never have happened to me before. I just wanted everyone to get out of our house. She left with her parents and our social worker, who to this day is our rock, helped us through the next few days. Our families were devastated. I can only say it felt that we were holding a wake for our son over the next few days, even though he was very much alive and crawling around, thinking it was great to have so much attention from all his favorite people. We spent our last days taking him to his favorite places.

He loved going to the park to feed the ducks. We planted a tree in his memory in our garden. We recorded some video footage of him over the last few days but to this day we have never watched it.

We didn't want him to go back to Dublin with strangers, so the morning he had to go back my brother-in-law drove us, his godparents came too. After sorrowful good-byes from our families we headed to Cúnamh. We went into that room, which is so hard to go back to in my mind right now, and we waited. She was late thank God, some precious time snatched with our baby. Then the moment came, our social worker entered the room and knowing that this was our final moments we kissed him and held on never wanting to let go. But we had to.......

It was horrendous, as I relive it now it doesn't get any easier. It is hard to write through tears. Days went by. He wasn't settling, we were giving our social worker any tips we could think of to pass on. He was missing us equally as much as we missed him. All I could think of was the pain he was in, what must he have thought of us not being there. It took a long time to get over it. Writing this opened up old feelings I never wanted to feel again. My husband says he can never revisit that room, that day again, in his mind. Actually on writing this I realise that none of us who traveled to Dublin that day and stood helpless in that room ever spoke about it again. We never revisited that scene, it was just too painful.

Thankfully, as I said, we got through it. We think of him still, especially birthdays. We have two fantastic kids now, who are a joy and a handful at times. And as I leave you now to go downstairs and sort out the row that is going on over who gets to put up the last witch for Halloween, I think, Jesus, we made it, we came through those dark, dark days and are now so happy, contented and full of hope for the future, we are a family and I treasure everyday we are together.

As for our first baby, who knows, maybe our paths might cross again, I always like to look at life as 'the glass being half full'.

Thank you Cúnamh

God Bless.

Sharon xx

To My Daughter

I once thought
Love was enough
But you tell me
You do not know who you are
When you look in a mirror
You say that girl in the red dress is not you
Neither are you the kid in the washed denim jeans

You pick up your mask on your way to school

You were chosen, but you were also left.

My Love is not enough
It makes you anxious
Used as you are to something different
But I will not give up
On those neural wayward paths
That flinch my touch and make love unsafe

I place the pieces of your mind carefully in a wheelchair,
With playfulness, acceptance, curiosity and empathy
And hope some day you will feel that hug
And find a place for love
In that too-controlled heart.

You think you are forgotten as soon as you walk out the door
Not knowing that you are indelibly written in the lives
Of mother, father, brother, birth mom
Forever
You think you are nothing
But we know what you are and not even your anger can take
that away

The beauty is in your photos of
2 ladybirds playing 'follow the leader' across your hand
Or the blue of that snail resting on the sand

Let me into your world of shame and anger and pain and help you
Name those feelings you don't even know you have
So that you can feel what we know
Love and warmth and joy

I am the safety net you do not want
When, like the apple from the tree,
You are ready to trust.

   Mom xxx

A FAMILY OF FIVE

'Love, Family, Growth, Reward and Identity'

McG. Family

THE EMPTY PRAM

It was by far the most nervous and excited I ever felt about anything in my life. I looked at my husband Mick, and could see by his expression, he felt the very same. Today, after an eight-year journey, we were about to meet our longed-for baby girl, Aoife.

It was a Monday lunch-time, and Dublin was thronged with business men and women walking with great energy and determination to reach their destination. I looked down at our brand new navy and brilliant white pram. As we battled through the crowds to make our way against the flow of people, the overwhelming feeling was how empty my pram looked, and the knowledge that in an hour or so it would be filled with our new daughter. What a feeling!

I hadn't slept properly since we received the call from Cúnamh on Friday afternoon to say that our time had arrived and that they had a lovely 8 week-old baby girl for us. My unspoken fear was what if I don't bond? What if she doesn't feel like my baby? What if she doesn't settle with us?

When we got to Cúnamh, Aoife hadn't arrived yet and we were brought upstairs to wait. She arrived twenty minutes later in a little yellow outfit and all my fears went out the window. Mick got a hold of her first. She beamed at us both and her beautiful brown eyes seemed to know us. She was a little beauty with fat chubby cheeks and a twinkle in her eye. I managed to pry her out of Mick's arms and was handed a bottle to feed her. She grabbed a hold of me with her tiny fist and that was that! Bonding complete! I kept smelling her and touching her not believing we could walk out the door with her. After lots of hugs, tears and thanks to the foster parents, we put our little girl into her lovely new pram and walked back down Grafton Street proud as punch with 'the empty pram syndrome' gone for good!

It was the start of a beautiful relationship which we have been blessed with. Aoife is a happy, confident and loving daughter who set the bar high for her sister who followed 18 months later and her three foster siblings 10 years after that. I send up a prayer of thanks to her Birth Mam on her birthday each year for the decision she made which led Aoife to our door.

Gráinne

The "Perfect" Adoptive Mother

The very first thing you have to realise is – there is no such thing as the "perfect" adoptive mother, just as there is no such thing as the perfect birth mother. In saying that though, I recognise that it won't stop you trying to be perfect. I know, because I have tried to be that person.

Going through the adoption process has caused me to question several aspects of my life but the most important, the one that's uppermost in my mind, is my status as a mother.

My son is 10 years old and since we agreed to be involved in an "open" adoption arrangement, he sees his birth mother regularly. He does not have any contact with his birth father thus far, and so he only has one "dad". For my husband there is no conflict, no other dad to be compared to. For me though, there will always be another mother, a constant reminder, a constant source of comparison, my competition in the mothering game. I cannot pretend she never existed. I can't control what she says to him, what she tells him about his adoption and I don't like not being in control.

Initially this really bothered me but over the years I have realised that just because my son is adopted does not make me any less his mother, than I am mother to my other children whom I gave birth to. I have become secure in my role as his mother.

After all isn't it the mothers who feed and hold their children, who wipe their tears when they cry, who pick them up when they fall, who sit up all night nursing them, bring them to hospital, dentists, football matches, birthday parties and pack them off to school. Doesn't a mother fight for the rights of her child when any injustice is done and put the needs of her children above all else? Over the past 10 years I have done all these things and I will continue to do all these things and more for my son and so, yes, I can now say I may not be perfect but I am most definitely his mother.

Hilary

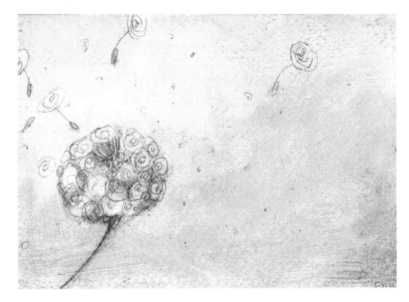

THE QUESTIONS WE ASK OURSELVES AS ADOPTIVE PARENTS

What is it like to live in our house, our home?

Do you feel comforted and loved everyday?

Are you growing emotionally and physically?

Will your memories comfort and sustain you when you grow up and move away from here?

Will the love and lessons you have learned in our house help you to be happy in your grown-up world and will they help you to influence the environment you live in, in small and great ways?

Will you look outside yourself and be aware of others' needs?

Will you remember the words of love we spoke?

"We love you all the way around the world, to the moon and back and always will"

We thank God everyday for the gift of our two children.

May the angels watch over us all and may our futures together be bright.

Tim & Trish

SON

We got the phone call one April afternoon.
A little baby boy.
We were over the moon.
And so the start of our journey began.
I studied your face as you held my hand.

On the 24th April you came home for good.
Very soon I adapted to motherhood.
You were such a happy little boy.
Never had I experienced such love and joy.

Your birth mum is our special friend.
A bond I hope will never end.
She gave you up, it was the right thing to do,
But she will never ever stop loving you.

We promise to give you a happy home.
A family to love all of your own,
We will be there for you everyday,
To protect and guide you along the way.

We blinked our eyes and now you're five.
What energy you have.
You're so full of life –
You started school on the first of September
A very special day for us to remember.

You have brought our family together.
We will love you always and forever.
So here's to all the years to come.
Thank you my darling, your loving mum.

Paul & Cathy

WHAT ABOUT ME?

He told his son that he had found his "real mum".

It's only words, language, not meant to wound.

But if she is "real", what about me?

That night in September, he on the phone, elated,

as he described his joy at this woman saying she was "his mother"

But if she was his mother, what about me?

Each meeting better, better than the last,

she so adoring, he so grateful.

Uncanny similarities they both agree.

She has proven herself seven times,

But, what about me?

How could you?

You told your son,

How could you?

Your "real mum" you said,

How could you?

Does that mean his "real gran",

How could you?

ADOPTION HAS ENRICHED OUR LIVES

After almost seven years of wanting a child and wanting to be a parent, the urgency of it all can take over, and blind you from what is in front of you. You become consumed by it all. You eat, drink and sleep adoption, while you go through the whole assessment process. Fortunately, our journey was a very positive one and having come through the other side as adoptive parents we want to share our experience of open adoption.

Open adoption is about dealing with your own insecurities, before you can move on to confront all the other issues that go with adoption. When you can get past that you are half-way to being a parent, you are already thinking as a parent. There are many pros and cons to open adoption, but the pros far outweigh the cons.

Twelve years on into open adoption, we as a family are communicating on a regular basis with the birth parents of both our children. As adoptive parents we hope we have given our children every opportunity to know their birth parents, and will continue to do so for however long.

Adoption has enriched our lives both as a couple and a family.

Aisling & Fintan

WAITING

She walked in, of slender build with long, dark hair framing her pale face. A supportive mother stood firmly at her shoulder. The air around us felt charged with passion and sensitivity. I forced myself to breathe, almost afraid to inhale any more emotion which might fill me to overflowing. As introductions were made, my feelings somersaulted, resigned to a back seat were our own disappointments, struggles with conception, tests and procedures, assessments and interviews – the weeks, months and years of waiting. These feelings which had initially bubbled frantically to the surface were quelled by the sacredness of the moment. This bright young woman swaddled in thoughts of her own journey over the past ten and a half months, might just be prepared to give us what we had been dreaming of for the past seven years. Could someone be so brave? Could someone show that much selflessness and love?

A brief stilted conversation was facilitated by the kindly social worker. Both parties outlined their individual journey which had led them to that formal drawing room in South Anne St. We each bared our fragile souls to the other - a small sacrifice in the greater scheme of things. Then on cue, the gentle girl in front of us passed us a little brown envelope of photographs - so symbolic. We stole a guilty look at those photos conscious all the while of what she must be feeling. Glancing furtively at her, I tried to gauge what she may have thought about us. But I couldn't see past the layers of emotion – mine and hers.

After the meeting the young woman was taken elsewhere for a chat. Us two were left alone. We just allowed all of the thoughts, words and feelings – spoken and unspoken, which had swirled around that high-ceilinged room, to settle. A while later the social worker returned. Soothingly she explained: ...... liked us a lot ...... unsure of her decision ...... needed more time. The word 'unsure' reverberated round and round the room beating in my ears until I could hear nothing else. Surely then I misheard the social worker saying that we could keep the photos. Of course we understood the need to be certain about such a life-changing decision. Beforehand we had definitely wanted the outcome of the meeting to be right for us. Now, having met this vulnerable, sincere birthmother, we desperately wanted what felt right for her also. Such conflict of emotion!

We drove home silently. Time stretched out endlessly in front of us. Our house seemed even quieter than usual if that were possible. Still warm from my grasp, the packet of photos was gingerly placed on the mantelpiece. Unable to invest a single further shred of emotion into that little packet of dreams, we dared not tempt fate by looking at them again. And then…..we waited.

P.S. Years later as I catch a glimpse of a red football shirt tearing toward me on a bike, I am fleetingly reminded of that emotional day. I offer a quick prayer of thanks to the Heavens and mutter to myself that 'some things are worth the wait'.

M&L

TWO WONDERFUL YOUNG PEOPLE

My husband and I started on our adoption journey some seventeen years ago when our beautiful daughter came into our family. She was joined by our wonderful son thirteen years ago. I cannot believe how quickly the years have passed and that our two little ones are now almost adults. Two wonderful young people whom we are so proud of and who have brought such joy and fulfilment to our lives.

We are so grateful for the life we have had and thank God we had the opportunity through adoption to share our lives with them and they with us. We used to worry about how best to give them a happy and successful life as their future is so important to us. However, the wisdom of age has brought us to a place where we now know that we live our lives going forward and make sense of it looking back.

We try to teach our children that contentment is wealth, to do their best and believe in themselves, never to be ashamed of failure, to learn from it and try again and never to boast about success. We also try to teach them not to be judgemental of others as we do not know the reason for their words or deeds, to not compare themselves to others, but recognise the value of good friends and to choose them carefully, to live with honesty and integrity and to try to find God and have him in their lives.

We finally hope that they will always know they are loved and cherished, that home is a safe place and that it will always be here for them. We also hope they stay connected with their biological parents as they also love them and wish only the best for them. We hope they give thanks and consideration to all relationships in their lives even some that are not straightforward.

I will end with a small poem given to me when I was about my daughter's age.

If you can't be a highway, be a lane
If you can't be a moon, be a star
It's not by size you win or lose
So be the best of what you are

Peggy

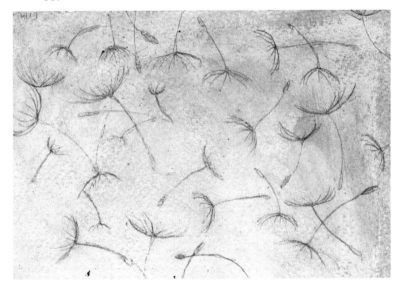

WHAT'S IN A NAME....?

There are no words or explanation to describe what it is like when you receive a phone call that begins with.... *"Hello Margaret, this is .... from Cúnamh. There is a little boy who would like to meet you........."*

Elation, pandemonium, joy, chaos, fear, all rolled into one and multiplied by a thousand. Margaret rings me immediately to tell me the news. The roller coaster of all roller coasters has begun. The next day we met our social worker. We listen to every word she says. We are like two wrecks, all over the place and thinking at a hundred miles an hour. Our social worker gives us all the details and answers to all our questions. She says that his name is Sam and that his natural mother, would like us to keep the name Sam. We have absolutely no objection at all. I am sure, like all other couples on the "waiting list", you hope some day that your dream of becoming a family comes through. It would be very naïve of us to say that we did not have a few boys' and girls' names for consideration like any other "expectant" parent. However, the name Sam had never come up on our list of names.

Anyway, we got Sam home. The first couple of months were a blur of cards, presents, nappies, flowers, bottles, formula, cots, soothers, buggies, monitors, callers, neighbours, family.....you name it...... but absolutely fantastic.

Then, one day, we were visiting friends of ours who have 3 children of their own. We had a great afternoon when my friend says "Well Sean, Sam is a great name for junior. Did you give him that name because ye are Sean and Margaret?" Well, if ever there was an instance of "Fate will have it", this was it. We never, ever had any concerns about the names of our children but isn't it just incredible how things work out!

Sam is now a typical, young fella, playing football and mad into having fun. He is Sam.

Margaret & Sean

ADOPTED PERSONS SHARE THEIR STORIES

5TH MARCH 2010

5th March 2010 is a day that has changed my life forever. That was the day I received a letter from Cúnamh to say that my birth parents had made contact with them about my wellbeing. It's a day I will remember for the rest of my life. I cried my eyes out; it was something I thought would never happen. Over the next few weeks I made contact with and met a social worker from Cúnamh. She explained the background to my adoption, within 10 minutes of meeting her I found out more than I had known in 38 years, where I was from, where I had been born and who I was, things that most people take for granted I suppose. The social worker explained that the normal procedure now was to exchange letters, but for no direct contact to be made just yet.

I received my first letter towards the end of March from my 'Mum and Dad'. It was a very emotional letter. It explained the circumstances of my adoption and that, the times being how they were, the decision had been made for my mum and dad. As time has gone past now, I do find it hard to take that my life was decided by someone I never have and now never will meet. I had been born in Holles Street Hospital, and had spent time in The Good Shepherd Mother & Baby Home in Dunboyne before my eventual adoption. As I read further I was told that I had 3 sisters and 2 brothers! In all my years of wondering, it never had occurred to me that I may have sisters and brothers.

After several letters back and forward, it was decided that I would meet my mum and dad on the 12th June 2010 in the county where they had come from. My wife and I travelled up on the 11th June, I was so nervous but excited at the same time. After a restless night, Saturday finally arrived. We were to meet at 11am, it couldn't come quick enough! We sat in the reception area of the hotel waiting; every car that pulled up raised me from my seat. At 11a.m. they arrived; I knew it was them the moment they stepped from the car. We walked to the hotel door and met them as they entered. It's a blur now, but I do remember that we all cried and hugged and then cried some more! We sat for a few hours chatting and answering the questions we all had. It was then decided that I would go and meet my two sisters and their families.

We followed my mum and dad's car for the ten-minute journey to my sister's house, where both were waiting. To say I was the proudest man on earth at that moment would be an understatement; these were my flesh and blood! We sat and chatted for a while, exchanging photos of my girls and exchanging stories of what had gone on in our lives, stories we all should have been part of, but were denied. We spent the weekend in Donegal and left on the Sunday. We agreed that we would bring our two daughters to meet their new family the following weekend. The following weekend we travelled to Donegal again. We went to my sister's house for a barbecue. When we got there I was told that we would be meeting a lot of my extended family, aunties, uncles, cousins, nieces, nephews etc; it was too much, too soon and I was completely overwhelmed. I found myself retreating into the background, and to be honest these "strangers" probably found me a bit strange!!

A few weeks later I decided I would travel to the UK to meet my other sister and two brothers. Again it was a very emotional time, I felt an instant bond with them. I don't know if they felt the same, but I certainly felt it. We spent the weekend together, again chatting and exchanging stories and photos. When I was leaving after the weekend I felt so sad that I just couldn't understand it, I was not an emotional person, but yet all these emotions came flooding out. I had to tell myself that this was only the start of things, but it was tough.

I am now 18 months into my reunion and there have been a lot of ups and downs in this period. I feel so much love for my brothers and sisters but have been disappointed with them too. Time can pass for weeks and I may not have any contact despite me sending texts or leaving messages on their phones. For me this has been one of the hardest things. I have started doubting that they want to bring our relationship forward and then have been questioning myself whether I am expecting too much. We have spoken about it and they have insisted that it wasn't the case, that it was the way they were and that they are always there if I need them.

I have recently attended a course run by Barnardos for adopted people. It has been of great help to me in understanding and appreciating the point I have reached in my reunion. Some people are still searching for answers to their lives and I have been fortunate to have met my birth family. For some this may never happen and that is the sad reality of being adopted. To be in a room with so many fantastic people that I could relate to was brilliant. I would highly recommend anyone taking the course.

Regarding my birth parents, I can say that we have a good relationship. We speak every few weeks. I still feel that we haven't dealt with the past. Our conversations still revolve around work, the kids and stuff like that. I do feel disappointed with my birth dad that he didn't support my mum through this; I do feel that if he had been stronger and stood by her, that things could have been different.

My adopted dad, my dad, died 9 years ago and I always wonder what he would make of all this. I do worry that I have upset my mum. She says that she is happy that I have found them and that as long as I don't get hurt, she is happy for me. My mum and dad and three brothers were the best thing that came out of this adoption. They have been and always will be the people who have made me the person I am today. Although you might feel that you are going to upset them, I think adopted people need to know where they come from, it's every human's basic right and adopted people should be no different. We will carry on getting to know each other and maybe some day everyone will have peace with what has happened, but no one said it would be easy!

Peter

A Day in the Life of an Adopted Person

It was Monday morning and I was off work for the day. How nice to be sitting on the hotel patio, overlooking Dublin Bay, having a coffee on this glorious, warm, sunny day. I was waiting for the social worker and my "new" brother to walk through the door to join me at any moment.... I had only learnt about him a couple of months ago.

Then, suddenly, I heard voices and I was introduced to him – we were both so nervous – we shook hands awkwardly – how do you greet a brother you have never met – two grown-up adults meeting for the first time....

We spent the day together – on what was possibly the warmest, calmest, sunniest day we had in August 2011. We sat on that patio and talked, hesitantly at first, then had more coffee, drove and had lunch together – then a walk down the pier – it seemed as if the whole world was in harmony with us – I have never seen the sea so calm.

The day rolled on – the chat rolled on – into a gallop – catching up as much as possible – there wasn't enough time (of course) but he met my daughter who had driven out to collect me that afternoon – another link made.

We organised to have the two families meet over the next couple of days of his stay here. Everyone we spoke to was so kind and accepting of our situation. There is a lot for which to be thankful.

But no-one just no-one knows what it is like to meet a full sibling after all these years – all they can do is look on – but my brother and I know – there is this new world now we have been lucky enough to have been allowed enter. And it is magic!

Think of all that has had to happen for a day like this to have come about... times have changed.... but there will always be a need for some kind of a support network to make endings like this possible.

Congratulations Cúnamh on all your successes – and thanks to you and your colleagues in counselling for your on-going good work.

Carol

A FAIRYTALE

Once upon a time there was a little baby girl born to a wicked Queen in a land in the South to which she was banished. This Queen had not always been wicked nor had she always had a secret to keep. But having met her particular dashing and handsome Prince quite a number of years before, she eventually had found herself heavily burdened, with what to some would have been a treasured gift. For her, the untimeliness of the occurrence and the distinct lack of a gold band prevented this from being the case! And so, the days were long for the Queen detained far from the comfort of her own small but prestigious kingdom - being kept from her wish to explore lands afar.

On the morn of the 10th nearing Yuletide - save the cold chill - all was well within the castle's walls. By evening time the white shouldered babe had announced her intended arrival in no uncertain terms. And so as the eighth bell chimed on that Monday after nightfall, the Queen was ensconced in her chambers holding her newly born babe aloft. She proclaimed aloud for all to hear - "Why Baby dear what fair skin you have. What blue eyes you have. What supple limbs you have. But, alas, how so like him you are!!"

"O Your Highness! Do not utter such words", the Lady in Waiting cried in response to her mistress's most obvious distress. "You are here for a while, but this sojourn will pass. For this child - I pledge - we will find a really good address!"

When six months had gone by, it was decided that the child would be moved to a place more fitting to the care of an infant. And so on a warm day in May a long journey was undertaken by the Queen and her party, which would culminate in the Queen abandoning her child and returning to her own land. This little girl was duly received with great joy and due care by a kindly couple who from that day forth would be her sole guardians and legal custodians. They swore to guide and protect, and to change her name!

And so they all lived for a while in the ever after – her birthright plundered but her welfare intact.

Jacqueline Finola Gwen

ALL OVER THE SHOP

I was born and adopted in 1956. Cúnamh contacted my mother in 2003 and we had one meeting in 2005. Since then there have been three phone calls to the agency from her, all motivated by a need to defend her position of absolute secrecy.

From our meeting in 2005 I got enough information to trace back into the ancestry of both my parents and I am very glad to have had that opportunity. But now I have exhausted the genealogical escape lines. After many hours spent in libraries, archives, presbyteries, graveyards etc I have collected a folder of documents – certificates of birth, marriage and death – which record the facts of my ancestors' lives. I have all the facts, but yet I know nothing. I only know where the bodies are buried.

But I have no real access to my living relatives. Even though I know where my mother lives, I may not visit her. Even though I have her number, I dare not telephone her. This is because she has never told her husband or her family. I am her secret. I do not want to be, but I am.

I have nothing to hide. I would be more than happy to be able to announce to the world: I am this woman's son; this man was my father. But I cannot do so. For my mother's sake – and for her sake only – I must remain silent, invisible, non-existent.

I have my own life to live. A life as simple and as complicated as any other. I am in many ways free, independent, comfortable, even privileged. But because I continue to be my mother's secret, my sense of identity remains muted and my origins have to be always hidden. Some part of me – the essence or core that non-adopted people may take for granted – is always suppressed. I am the proverbial can of worms.

At 52 years of age, I have three grown-up children, each older than my mother was when she found herself pregnant. I am older now than my mother's parents were in 1955 when she fled to England to deal with her crisis. Now I am the father of a 5-year-old girl for whom this grandmother just does not exist. I don't see that I have any choice but to keep this information from my daughter, but it means that the charade of secrecy continues. I am not just the object of secrecy, but a participant in the process. Not only must I carry with me someone's secret, I am that secret incarnate.

And what am I to do if my mother dies? Am I to appear after a decent interval of mourning and reveal myself to her family? How would they feel? Wouldn't it be better if she could bring herself to tell them herself? I certainly think so. But I doubt if she will or can.

Sometimes I think that people imagine that we live in enlightened times. A world of forgive-and-forget, of instant confession and absolution, where closure and moving-on are merely functions at our fingertips. Not so for people embroiled in the absurd secrecy cycle of adoption. On one occasion my mother spotted me in the supermarket and she swung her trolley round and re-surfaced at the farthest corner of the shop. How did she feel? How did I feel? We were all over the shop: an apple-cart and a can of worms.

Pádraic

A whole new world was opened up to me

I was reminded last Sunday, while playing golf, that 12 years ago, almost to the day, I let a happy scream (more like a yahoo) out of me on a golf course in Tenerife, my social worker had found my mother and she was alive and well and living in Boston and yes she would meet me....but (there's always a but) not in Boston, and only on her terms...you see she had told nobody, not a single person, not her 5 brothers, or her 2 sisters, or her parents, or friends, not even my father, and very definitely not her present husband (not my father and now deceased) and their 4 daughters (my sisters). So it was agreed that on one of her many visits to Ireland, she would meet me, the baby she gave up for adoption 50 years earlier.

That meeting never took place, for whatever reason she decided it would never happen. Three years later she developed Alzheimers, and all subsequent letters from my social worker in Cúnamh remained unanswered.

I had almost made my mind up to leave her in peace and respect her wishes but every year on February 28th she would surface in my mind, as I'm sure I did in hers. That was the day that a very frightened and alone woman gave birth to me in England .... so years later, after constant nudges and reminders of my "wishes" and my "rights" by my own wife, I started again to pester my social worker to send more letters and make more phone calls. In the meantime I had no trouble getting my birth certificate from England, but information can be a burden, if you can't do anything with it.

The hope was that, now knowing my ma had Alzheimers and was in the care of one of my 4 sisters in Boston, that one of the girls would open the letters and reply. Bingo, that's what happened. Initially they thought it was some sort of scam, but my sister Fiona called my social worker, and all was revealed. We then had to wait till she told the other girls that they had a brother.

The wait was short and the reaction unbelievably positive ... like the next day, they called "when can you come over"? was the first question, and "you will stay with us and we'll have a party," etc, etc. So on 17th October 2011, 12 years after I started looking, Carmel and I landed at Logan airport to an emotional first meeting with my 4 sisters, followed by a tearful first meeting with my 88 yr old mother. She obviously hadn't a clue who I was, but as the days progressed, we took a "wait and see" approach and on day 3, when we were alone, and she let me into "her" world, the secret was shared. I wouldn't sell that moment for a million dollars. We spent 8 great days in Boston, being spoiled and pampered, and getting to know my new family. Plans are already afoot for reunions ...with sisters and extended family.

On reflection the relationship with my mother will, because of her condition, be limited, but a whole new world has opened up for me and my sisters and their kids and mine.

What happened next....

Shortly after my return from Boston, while still on a high, I decided to continue the search for my birth father. I had found out his name from my searching in England and knew that he was a male nurse back in the 50's. This turned out to be a great help. The unbelievable coincidence is, he had been working and living in the town I grew up in with my adoptive parents. Sadly he didn't know I existed.

He later moved to Manchester, where he married and had 4 lovely daughters and a son. Cúnamh came out trumps again, once we were sure we had the right man, contact was made with the family.

Again, after a cautious and suspicious early contact, all dealt with very professionally by my social worker, I received 2 emails and a phone call in early January 2012. The opening line of my sister's email was heart warming.

"Can I first start by saying how great it is to have a new brother?"

The same welcome came from another sister's informative and warm email and then a phone-call from my brother who wanted to hop on a plane and come over for a pint in Dublin.

The sad news was that my dad had died back in the 80's, aged 58, of colon cancer, never knowing I existed, and all his brothers and sisters had died at a relatively young age.

So the good news is I have come from being an only adopted son to now being part of an extended family of 4 sisters in the USA, and 4 sisters and a brother in Manchester, all of whom have welcomed me with open arms, and nowhere was the term "half-brother" or "step-brother" used.

I also, now, have a medical history from both of my natural parents, and a budding new family relationship developing on both sides of the Atlantic.

I hope this story gives hope to anyone in a similar situation, especially if it's not going as well as you'd like ... don't give up, your social worker and other staff are there to help you, and as my social worker said to me on many occasions..."*Paddy, it's so right*".

I will be eternally grateful to my social worker and her co-workers in Cúnamh, for the sensitive and professional job they did in locating and reuniting me with the woman who gave me my first breath and with both my families.

Thanks and respect.

Paddy

AN OPEN LETTER TO MY BIRTH MOTHER

A commemoration to Unspoken Words and to an Unacknowledged Lineage

Dear Ann,

Your Ireland was a fledgling nation; a post-colonial phenomenon with all the inherent insecurities. Bunreacht na hÉireann was contemporaneous to your birth. This was a Constitution that sought to make it hard for women to be anything other than married mothers or nuns – even these roles bore prejudicial treatment. Five years earlier in 1932, the honour of a Eucharistic Congress hosted on these shores poised on the precipice of nascent nationhood, saw a legion of all-male compatriot political and clerical hierarchy flaunt their newly-proved autonomy. Amongst the general populace however, poverty, disease, and all associated social ills were rife, and those who lived above the breadline survived to a large extent, in terror of their circumstances changing. Weaving their merry way then between their fellow oft-begrudging-countrymen and the old-guard English gentry, the indigenous elite were shuffling to take their positions, to establish their status, to show where the power lay – to become recognised once again as rightful leaders of their communities.

By your 18th year in 1955, you had left a Catholic boarding school education here to start a course in a third-level college in the UK. Your family could afford this privilege easily. The ancestral home was a big house on the hill overlooking the town. A family of nurses, you vowed not to be one. Small town living meant little fun and many prying eyes. Emigration rates were high for females at the time, as opportunity and independence lay beyond Erin's shores. You were the high-spirited one in your house, or so your Mother dubbed you. You were like your alcoholic father always seeking adventure. This was the man with the rich legacy whose business affairs were administered from the bed. He had replaced exotic India's 'ex-pat' lifestyle for the rurality of a large landed country home, a Papal dispensation and a match-made marriage to a relative of some means. You loved him dearly though – the man who instructed you all to come bid him goodnight with a glass of whiskey concealed on your person, deftly hidden from his wife's moral eyes.

At 21 you gave birth for the first time–and this next piece you recount with reluctance- in a Mother and Baby Home across the waters where you learned the art of scrubbing the cracks in the marble floor tiles with a nailbrush. It was far from this that you were reared! Your mother brought you home in high summer. She was never the same. You couldn't have been either. It left its indelible mark. You subsequently had a breakdown and then spent your time at home helping her to run the house and to mind your errant Father. You heard him taunt her and witnessed his lack of regard.

It is no wonder you sought distraction then. He was made welcome in the homestead - seen as worthy of its care. Not like the local boys who your Mother forbade you to see. He was 'one of our own'. While enjoying a reputation locally as an unconventional scholar, he was a loved and respected member of Ireland's coterie of men above reproach. You were almost 26 when I came on the scene – your 'replacement baby'. He was 43 by now, and was to let you down. "No backbone", you said, "like many an Irish man". Talked of marriage and then reneged. But not before he donned his other cap. It was he who liaised with the Adoption Agency, and it was he who communicated with your family on your account. His role was to intercede for the woman of illrepute. You were the girl who had given in - surrendering to the call of 60's Ireland. He was photographed attending Balls and meetings in Dublin at weekends. It is reported that he spoke passionately in halls around the country during the week, while finding time to teach, to study diligently and to write prolifically, on the broad range of subjects that engaged his mind.

All the while, we were negotiating the strict routines of the Mother and Baby Home. You had a period of six months to fulfill this time, as this was your 'second fall' after all. This then was a reason to stay in touch – as well as loving him, you were obliged. What did a man of his brilliance see in a girl like me, you often wondered? Your secret family – at once a Father, a cousin and a son and a daughter. A confused situation surely – a real threat to the status quo. On completion of the last forms for my adoption which he advised you to fill, you left for England again, but this time never to return to live. Your trips home thereafter were short and infrequent. A second child gone from your care.

You knew patriarchy Irish-style only too well. You did not choose therefore to become either a married mother or a nun for that matter – you had seen enough of them! The old maid prototype did not suit you at all - most unbecoming... You were London-bound. This was the place for a new style of being – it was also home to those with a past. London in those days was so exciting. It was the place to be, you told me. You adjusted and played the role of the care-free city-woman well, only agreeing to marriage at 45, when all excuses were exhausted and childbearing was most definitely not in the plan. You were a favourite Aunt by this time I have been told.

But how did you smooth the ragged edges of your life's path? What of 'cellular memory'? - 'the ancestral voice'? 'the descendants right to know' - a cacophony of muffled sounds to be ignored, to be phased out. Ann, why is it that you felt so compelled to conceal this crumpled secret all the days of your life? It is too late for me to find out – a missed opportunity. My loss and yours... Your window of time has shattered and fallen now, leaving a myriad of multiple meanings to plane and shapes to confound. I know you suffered physically as your life drew to its end. Was this a genetic inheritance or could it have been the result of an alternative life repressed? MS, heart attacks, and finally cancer at 68, the final destroyer. Your truth got buried deep.

He lived a full life bound to his craft. He was a genius, his obituary claimed, but not a maverick like so many of his ilk - always a lively conversationalist and kind. A seer, a far-seer... And what came of him? At 71 he had a stroke that stole his voice – a great instrument of power by all accounts. He survived it seems, in a pathetic silence, without even the comfort of his beloved writing as a medium of communication in his final eight years. How did he reconcile his beliefs with his actions I often wonder?

Honours were bequeathed upon him before his final demise. It seems that history – 'auld history' as he would have it- judged his achievements well, although clearly, not all have come to light!

You, Ann, bestowed the most cherished gift of all - complicit, implicitly...

Your contribution was silence.

Yours truly,

Your baby girl grown up

So Loved

I am adopted and so loved,

People who hear say so sorry,
But they should say so loved,

I have birth parents and their families,
I am so loved,

I have had a foster family and their friends,
I am so loved,

I have an adoptive family,
I am so loved,

I am so wanted,
I am so loved,

Adoption isn't sorry,
It is so loved.

K

An Tost ag Réabadh

Faoi rún, faoi cheilt
Ón uaigh
ata sí,
ag macallaigh ...
ag cogarnaíl
faoin
saol
sáite
i ré atá thart.
A luachanna
ag tochailt
go smior tríd
sochaí
galánta, ach-
mímhacánta

Ceacht le foghlaim-
Impionn si orm
"Cuir caoi air", a deir sí
Réitigh é,
Déan cinnte
 go bhfuil an ciorcail
ag dúnadh.
An tAthaontú
Slán
ón ngaoth nimhneach
diphréamhaithe
a thugann an t-easpa" ....

Jacqueline Finola Gwen

INTERRED IN A GRAVE IN GLOUCESTER

Secrets she's hiding...
The tomb's an echo.
Whispering
a life
of
bygone days,
Of
variant
Values
burrowing
rampant and relentless,
A Ravaging Sodality-
Virtue's game.

Lesson-learning- for
Loss
She implores.
"Mend it", she says.
Resolve.
Our circle
Renewed
Our
Lineage
delivered
from
the winds of Ruin-Spoil's
fragmented absence.

Jacqueline Finola Gwen

Note: writer would like it acknowledged that these poems
were conceived or "cumatha" in Irish. The English versions are
adapted and translated from the original Gaeilge.

FÍODÓIR BEANNAITHE: IS TÚ MO PHEACA

Sniomhtha ag máthair – nár thug,
nár thuig,
Scaoil sí uaithi a breith
'Bréidín an druis'-
Meon
Corp
is Anam
Múnlaithe
agus
Fáiscthe ag
An Oide –

Í cleachtaithe air

An chéad uair...
Arís
an dara babhta-
Sliocht anois ann
don Saoi
gan locht,
Reacaire
Scartha
ó gach ceangal.

Aineolach...
Tréighthe ...
Gan tuiscint...
Gan tús
Lár
nó críoch-
Finscéal...

Leanbh faoi méachan ama

Jacqueline Finola Gwen

WORDS-MADE FLESH..HER POISONED CHALICE

Mother-weaver, Secret-bequeather,
Unknowing, Unforeseen,
Cast off at birth
a Material lust-
Intellect,
Body
and
Soul
Moulded
and
Formed
By her Cloth Master
Knowing only his Design.

First time
And then
A Second Round.
Fruits of her loom
For
The Shaman -
A storyteller
Unfastened
From all ties

Innocence
Abandoned ..to
No reveal
No beginning, middle, or end
No tale
Birth weighted by time.

Jacqueline Finola Gwen

Note: writer would like it acknowledged that these poems
were conceived or "cumatha" in Irish. The English versions are
adapted and translated from the original Gaeilge.

BUT WHERE ARE YOU FROM, ORIGINALLY?

Summer holidays were endless. They were spent at Omey strand, a vast expanse of sand and rock-pools, which would be revealed twice a day, by the retreating tide. At low water, an enigmatic route to the island, a causeway in the sand, was marked by rusting posts, like a string of lollipops, stretching away into the distance.

The weather always seemed to be windy and sunny, with enormous Connemara skies, racing in from the Atlantic Ocean. I remember the scents of the island, fragrant with wild thyme in the meadow grass, the sharp tang of iodine, from great whorls of seaweed, hurled up onto the shore from the relentlessly churning sea. There were irresistable treasures to be discovered for a young girl: terns' nests hidden amongst the stones, wild orchids, a holy well, festooned with fading rosaries, ribbons, coins, miracalous medals.

The strand linked Omey to the rest of the world. It was strewn with tiny granite islands, knobbly mounds, like upturned puddings, sculpted by age and the sea. They were dotted with perfectly orbicular sea pinks, their miniature flowers, bobbing in the breeze, clinging into crevices, where they sought out pockets of rainwater-sodden soil. These were small worlds for me, waiting to be explored.

I loved to abandon my wellingtons, musty and damp from their frequent, unintentional dunking below the waterline. My bare clenching toes snapping off tendrils of samphire grass, its pungent lemony, sea-scent, filling the air as I skipped, barefoot, between the pools and those pink and green and silver-coloured lands. It was a faraway place, another world, in my imagination, a playground, a place to dream.

This is where I recall my mother was happiest. She drank in this untamed beauty, content with the simplicity of having little to do and endless days to do it. I can picture her still, unperturbed by us, her brood of three, as she pottered about, searching for mussels in their inky-black shells, hidden behind curtains of seaweed. Foraging for cockles at the very edges of the strand, she would return purposefully with a rake, entreating assistance to fill a bucket. They would appear later that evening in a creamy seafood soup, clanking deliciously together in their butterfly-opened shells.

I vividly recall one particular day, tucked away in one of my hideaways, idly picking off the grains of sand that had dried onto my feet. I inspected my double freckle, a small, distinctive birthmark, that lay just above the smallest toe on my left-foot.

"I wonder, did she ever examine it, in the same way that I am doing so now? Maybe she put it there, at least, she couldn't have, but perhaps it's a mark, a sign she could use to identify me, if she ever came to look for me?"

I shocked myself with the sudden realisation that I had drifted into forbidden territory. To consider another life that might have been, to think of my birth mother. It seemed inexplicably taboo, so much so, that I hadn't dared to do it, even in the privacy of my own head.

I glanced around uncertainly, half-expecting her to appear against the skyline, coming towards me across the beach. The thought of her unnerved me, for some reason, and I shivered in the summer breeze. Yet there she was, moving towards me, a figure looming, larger now, dressed in a sari which whipped around her frame, catching her ankles in the breeze. She gazed at me with a menacing frown.

"Why have you conjured me up? Why have you brought me here?"

Although I knew she wasn't real, I couldn't actually see her, and she wasn't really talking to me, I was utterly shaken. What did she want from me? Had she come to claim me? Then, as quickly as she had appeared, she vanished again. My family in the near distance, seemed to be completely unaware of this startling visitor. I searched the sands that stretched into the shimmering haze, as far as the horizon. She was gone.

I remember it now as clearly, as if it had happened yesterday. It felt like releasing a long, deep exhalation. In that breath of time, I understood what it meant for me to be adopted. I experienced the sense of loss, bewilderment and displacement that remains with me still. I had another mother once, and must 'belong' to another, entirely different, family?

It felt disloyal, almost a betrayal, to think like this, a little threatening, an inkling of excitement tinged with fear. Who were these people, this unknown family, a nation, race, from which I came, yet knew nothing of? Would they ever want to know me? Would they ever come to find me? Did she really hate me? Why did she leave me?

Growing up as the only black child in a mixed race family, I was always afflicted with being different. When we were quite young, we were told that we were adopted. I was the dark-skinned one. It was explained to us that I was 'fully Indian'. My white-skinned brother was described as being 'half' Indian, having an Irish mother and an Indian father. My white sister, presumably of white parentage, though this was not elaborated, was told that she came from England. It was that black and white; literally.

I always felt I was the one who stood out, unlike my siblings, for whom, I felt, no explanations were necessary. They were white: therefore they were acceptable. If it weren't for me, and my dark skin, no-one need have ever known that any of us were adopted.

How could I identify with being 'fully' Indian when thismeant absolutely nothing to me? I had no reference points, other than it made me different. I felt a shame, I bore a secrecy that I didn't understand. I felt that I wasn't properly one of the family and I couldn't be Irish either. It brought with it a deep-rooted sense of 'not belonging'. I envied my brother and sister their pale skin, their ability to blend in, sparing them the labels, the questions for which I had no answers.

"Nigger, you're a dirty black bastard". "Why are you brown"?

I learned to live with my tormentors. I came up with some snappy retorts, though mostly, I just wanted to curl up inside,and die with mortification. The names, they came with the territory, though each time they were hurled at me, they cut like a knife. I pretended that it didn't matter, that I didn't care what they called me. On the outside I was happy, successful, I did well at school. I was determined to prove to everyone, especially myself, that it didn't matter.

"But where are you from originally"?

The innocuous question: asked of me by children, well-meaning adults, then later, friends, colleagues, and often, complete strangers. For me, it was worse than the insults because I had no answer, either for myself or to satisfy the curiosity of others. I dug down and buried it deep. The essence of who I was, twisted tortourously inside me, burning like a slow fire.

The birth of my eldest daughter, my known first biological relative, was what was eventually to precipitate my search. Holding her in my arms for the first time, I knew that I loved her, unconditionally. As it is with newborns, her eyes, with their ageless wisdom, gazed through me, seeking out my very soul. I sensed the fathomless connection to those who had gone before her, before me. I was compelled to find answers to the questions that had beguiled me, to overcome the fear, the belief that I had no right to delve into my own past.

There had been many secrets, kept, untold. Whose interests do they serve? Whose voices are silenced by adoption? My birth story came tumbling out, Irish woman meets Indian medical student. The subsequent choices that had been made for me, and their consequences on my life, began to unfold.

All along, there had been one simple, immeasurable ommision. I had never been told that I had an Irish mother, that I was half-Irish, half-Indian. Every child, every person, has a right to their own identity, for their voice to be heard. I sometimes still feel that I am voiceless.

Secrecy and shame are no longer the foundations upon which adoption is based today. However, for those of us who grew up in a mono-cultural, conservative society, which deferred absolutely to the authority of the Catholic Church, their impact is life-long and spans the generations. Why do adoptees, adoptive parents and birth parents have so much difficulty speaking to each other? Why is it uncomfortable for me to explain how I feel about my adoption to my children?

My mother died before she got a chance to meet my children. I have been reunited with my birth mother. For all of us her role of grandmother is a treasured one. I have linked the generations, yet I feel somehow disconnected, the link that was lost.

I am on a journey to regain a lost, cultural identity. I have brought our children, stood at the graves of our ancestors, read their names, heard their histories. Although they never knew us, I can begin to sense a connection, with my ancestry, this land and my history. For me, it is priceless.

"In all of us there is a hunger, marrow-deep, to know our heritage — to know who we are and where we have come from. Without this enriching knowledge, there is a hollow yearning . . . and the most disquieting loneliness."

Alex Haley, Author of Roots

An extract from a novel by Sarah

DISCOVERING WHO I AM

I have just returned recently from England following one of many visits with my mother. She is in her eighties now and thankfully in very good health.

In my early 50's and driven by nothing more than curiosity I decided to try to discover where my natural parents had come from. I always knew that I had been adopted at 6 months and had been christened in Dublin. I had occasionally thought about doing this over the years but out of a sense of loyalty to my adoptive parents never pursued it while they were alive. I had a very happy upbringing and had no emotional void I needed to fill. I was just interested to see what I could discover. Through initial contact with Cúnamh I quickly found out that my mother had come from Ulster and was still alive and living in England. My father, who had lived in Connacht, sadly had died unmarried in the mid-1990's. They had met when my mother went to work for his family in the early 1950's and had begun a relationship together. My mother became pregnant but circumstances dictated that marriage to my father was not an option at that time and she had to leave for Dublin where I was born.

My mother cared for me in Dublin until I was six months old but eventually had to place me for adoption. She wrote to Cúnamh's predecessor after my adoption asking them to "let me know how he is, how I would love to see him again". It was to be more than fifty- three years before that was to happen.

Having moved to England to try to forget and move on with her life she met an Irish man whom she married and had a family with. Until Cúnamh contacted her a few years ago she had never told her family or friends about this period in her life. It must have been a very lonely secret for her to have kept all those years.

As you would expect all contact had to be on a consensual basis and Cúnamh was initially the conduit for all communication and only withdrew when everyone was comfortable and it was considered no longer necessary. We have been happily flying solo ever since.

On my father's side I have met his last surviving sibling, my uncle and also my cousins and have been very much accepted into the family. Family resemblances became immediately apparent and I have discovered that my father and I had many interests in common which explains a lot. Naturally I would like to have met him but unfortunately that was not meant to be.

Not surprisingly my mother had no photographs of their times together but had kept the negative of one of my father which she had taken all those years ago. I now have a print and am glad that they had been close before she had to move away.

There is a lot more to my story than would be appropriate to write here but it is all positive and I am very glad that I eventually decided to trace my family background and without hesitation would encourage anyone thinking about it to do so.

I would like to record my sincere thanks to Cúnamh for facilitating it all and for the very sensitive and professional manner in which they dealt with everything.

Des

FOSTERED

My name is Dermot. I am 65 years old. I was born in the Coombe Hospital in Dublin. As I was born out of wedlock my mother had to give me up for adoption. I was fostered by two people who lived in Co. Wicklow. I always referred to them as Mam and Pop. As well as fostering me, they fostered two other children and also raised two biological children.

It was when I started going to school that I realised that I was being fostered as my surname was different to Mam and Pops' surname. Growing up in rural Ireland was quite tough as the school, church and shops were two miles away from where we lived. Furthermore our home was situated at the top of a very steep hill. I recall walking the 4- mile round trip to the shops on a Saturday with Mam, and then doing it again on a Sunday morning to attend mass which started at 8.30 a.m. so it was always an early start!

As we were growing up we could see that there was never a lot of money at home so my brother and I started to work for farmers on a Saturday and during the school holidays to try to earn a few shillings. We did that for a number of years until we left school to work full-time. Looking back I cannot remember Mam and Pop ever going on a holiday or going away for a day together. I think that their whole life was dedicated to working and to rearing their children. They were great people. You could call them "the salt of the earth". I'm sure that you could say the same of a lot of people back in those days. Mam and Pop didn't grow to be very old and I often thought that it had a lot to do with the hardship they endured during their lives. However, they always seemed happy and content with the life they had.

Later on in life I often thought about my birth parents and wondered whether I should try to trace them, but I always seemed to get "cold feet". However in 2010 I decided that I would try and trace their whereabouts and find out about their families. First of all I wrote to Cúnamh as I had been fostered through the agency in 1946. Later I had a meeting with a social worker who was extremely helpful throughout my search.

My two half-brothers were traced and I have now met them and their families. Our mother had passed away in 1988. My mother's brother, who was 89 years old, told me that he knew that his sister had had a third child but he never told my half-brothers about me. My brother's daughter told me that finding out about me was one of the best things that happened to their family. I think that that was one of the nicest things that was ever said to me.

This is just a small section of the search for my roots and I am blessed that it had such a happy ending. However, I am well aware that there are a lot of people who go in search of their roots who are not so fortunate as to have a happy ending.

I am very grateful to Cúnamh for the wonderful help given to me throughout my search.

Dermot

ABANDONED

Having to surrender a baby for adoption due to financial reasons, social stigma and ecclesiastical dogmatic principles during the twentieth century is truly tragic and sad for a country in this present day.

For the adopted person there is the missing out on a birth mother's care. Your sixth sense, a hunch, a gut feeling, telling you what is, is not really, pondering over your doubts. Not all is revealed, something is not quite right, something you just can't put your finger on. One hasn't heard all the facts. Something in the back of your mind telling you there's something quirky about all this (a glint of an eye, a crooked smile). All these thoughts racing through your head while in your teens.

You feel forsaken, abandoned, rejected, isolated, outcasted, secluded, deserted, despondent - in short, abandoned.

You feel like you are living a dual life, have an alias name, you could have had this life but you had that one, you were called this name but were given another after adoption. You feel a lack of trust and suspicion of other people. Then you find out later all about it and who you really are.

Then there may be a reunion with your birth mother, her husband and siblings should they be present. It can give rise to guilt, shame and regretfulness. A third party (social worker) negotiates between the birth mother and the adopted person in order to facilitate a contact.

You try to understand and come to terms with the surrendering of an innocent baby. You think about what it must have been like for your birth mother at that time, in that period in history, the 1950's. You think about the grief and sorrow she must have endured. The secrets that were kept to herself. The denials and acts of pretence she kept and endured throughout her life. You think of the deprivation for all concerned.

With this comes understanding, healing and forgiveness from it all.

My adoptive parents were the most kind, giving and thoughtful parents one could ever have. I have great respect and love for both of them and what they lived through from the 1920's onwards. With what I know now they have probably given me a better life than my birth mother could ever have given me at that time. I am sincerely grateful and in their debt. I have unlimited love and respect for them both. God bless yea.

Stephen

"I KNOW"

I found out that I was adopted when I was 14 years old after finding adoption papers in my parent's room. I found my brother's adoption papers first, to which I went into total denial. For days after I would go back to just look at my brother's papers, this went on for a while. I started to become fascinated by it all but then one day I dug deeper, and there under my brother's papers were my own adoption papers.

I found the whole experience very upsetting. I felt as though my stomach had been ripped out. Why wasn't I told? Is this real? Who am I? Where did I come from? I did not want it to be real. For days my head felt heavy and I didn't have the courage to say that I knew. I suppressed it for over 13 years. Every so often I would wonder about my biological mother and father and why did my adoptive parents never tell me. I had various reasons of course. One being that they must have told my brother and he couldn't handle it and that was why he became destructive with alcohol and drugs. This for me was what I believed happened; my parents feared that if they told me about being adopted that I would go down the same path as my brother. I think I took some solace in that. Even at a very young age I was able to place myself in their shoes and try to understand why they never told me.

It wasn't until I was 27 years old that I finally had the courage and strength to tell my parents that I knew and I had known since I was 14 years old. It came about when the adoption register was in the news. I had to find out which agency was involved in my adoption. When the letter arrived in the postbox my heart stopped. It reaffirmed that I was adopted. I think even though I had found the papers all those years ago I somehow thought it was still unreal. There in black and white was the name Cúnamh. I was adopted and that was that.

During this time I had been seeing a counsellor and she found it strange that I was never told. I had been working through all the suppressed feelings that I had kept in me for nearly 13 years. Looking back I really don't know how I managed to do reasonably well in school, go to college and seemingly have a normal balanced adolescence with all that in the back of my mind. I made an appointment to go into Cúnamh and when I was brought into the room, the window was open, I could hear Grafton Street, all the flower sellers, people having lunch, people chatting having coffee. It felt very surreal. I had passed this building many times as a child, a teenager and as a young woman and never knew there was a file about where I came from sitting in their filing cabinet. As the social worker from Cúnamh read my information, I cried and cried. I could hear life outside but inside that room I was hearing for the first time where I was born, how much I weighed, my original name, my mother's name, my father's name, what baby food I liked and the circumstances around my adoption. That day really shook me.

I cried like a baby for the next few days. I was extremely disoriented, lost and isolated. It was obvious to my parents that something was up with me, they tried numerous times asking was I okay. I still hadn't the courage to say 'I know'. I would practice in the mirror the conversation that I needed to have with them. This went on for days. I was scared, confused and lonely. I was in the sitting room and I must have said it a hundred times in my head 'just say it now, say it'. Then I did. I said to my mam 'I know'. She just looked at me and she knew. I said 'I know about being adopted and I know about my brother too'. She just hugged me. I cried then. The big secret was out. No more holding on to it. It was out and it felt good.

It's nearly four years since that conversation and a lot has happened, I have found new information about my biological parents and most importantly my medical history. I was right, my parents never told me as they feared I would end up going down the same path as my adopted brother. I have attended numerous courses for adopted people. I speak very openly about adoption in my parent's house. No more secrets, no more 'big elephants in the room', no more denial. It's been quite a rollercoaster journey, ups and downs, tears and laughter, but I am always moving, to what I don't know, but the feelings are balanced and that keeps me strong. I would like one day to meet my biological parents, to see how they look, I suppose, and also to say that I am well and that I was cared for and looked after, that my life is full of wonderful things.

Melissa

I STARTED TO FEEL DIFFERENT

It all started for me when I was around nine or ten. I started to feel different........ different in the sense that I didn't fit in. That went on for the next forty years until at the age of fifty I found out I was adopted. I had never seen the long version of my birth certificate and as my wife was going to get one for herself I asked her to get mine. That was how I found out. The secret had been kept from me for all those years. When I found out I had feelings of happiness and sadness. Happy that all the feelings I had of being different wasn't me going mad and sadness that the family that I grew up with and looked after me were not my real family. I know that might sound ungrateful but that is just the way I felt at the time.

When I found out it not only affected me it also affected my wife and my two sons who have helped me to where I am today.

I have spent the last eight years searching for my birth mother. When I started to search I went to Cúnamh as they were the organization that handled my adoption all those years ago. I met with a lovely lady who has helped me a great deal. I can't thank her enough for all the help and support she has given me. I will never get to meet my birth mother as she passed away earlier this year. I have got a lot of letters that were on my file and from those letters it seems that she was a very caring and loving person who was in a very difficult situation all those years ago.

Through Cúnamh I have made contact with my birth mother's brother who is a lovely man. I have met him several times and it's like I have known him all my life. He has been able to give me a lot of information about my mother's life both before and after I was born. She went on to be married and have three more children and I hope some time in the future to meet them.

Nick

I was adopted in Ireland

My arrival at 9lbs in the summer of 1956 cannot have been a happy event for those who were present. My mother was to be forced because of the time and religious beliefs of the country to give away her first-born daughter. She went on to give away three other healthy daughters. I live in the absolute knowledge that my own beloved daughter will care for me in my dotage without hesitation. The agony of having to give away your child and to never have the comfort of knowing that certainty or indeed the utter joy and moments of pride at your child's little steps and achievements through their school years and beyond is unimaginable to most of us lucky enough to have a guilt-free relationship and give birth without judgement in a time and country free from prejudice.

Following my successful kidney transplant in 2004 my wonderful sport-loving son was discovered to carry the genetic disorder which can lead to renal failure. Without this diagnosis I would never have discovered through the following correspondence how truly loved I was by the parents with whom I was placed.

14th July 1956 from Miss C (social worker)

"You will be glad to hear that at long last we have another suitable baby for you and I hope that all will go well this time. Her name is DF and she was born on the 14th June. She really is a lovely baby and as her background is very similar to S we feel she would fit in well with your home. We have had her examined by the doctor and he has pronounced her perfectly fit in every way. I look forward to hearing from you and we can arrange to place this baby with you as soon as you wish".

20th July from BL (my mother)

"We are all very excited about the baby. May we fetch her on Friday 3rd August? Today fortnight? By that time my mother

in law will be well settled in and nana back from holiday. In
great haste so please excuse the scribble. Thank you for all your
help and patience!"

27th July from BL

"Thank you for your letter. I will fetch the baby (from you?) at
about 3pm. That will give her time to have her 2oz bottle and
she will probably sleep on the way home. I will bring a Karri
(sic) cot for her and can also bring clothes if you like".

31st July 1956 from BL

"I am afraid I have to change plans. I wonder if I might fetch
the baby at 10.45 instead of the afternoon on Friday. I find I
must be back here for the afternoon to look after my mother in
law. If it is not alright could you leave a message on Thursday
evening? Otherwise I will be with you at 10.30".

Note with feeding regime given to BL

Four and half level measures of Cow and Gate with 5ozs of
water and half a spoon of sugar every three hours.
Four ozs water with spoonful of glucose and half a spoonful of
sugar twice a day between feeds.
Due feed at 12 o'clock.

Undated postcard from BL

"Have just sent off a little parcel with the baby's clothes as I
feel your need is very great with the good work you are doing.
She has been a bit unsettled but I think is beginning to be more
at home now. Anyway we are getting very attached to her".

The final letter was sent on the 1st December from BL

"*Dear Miss C*

I have been meaning to write every day your letter made me feel awful. You will I know be glad to hear that J is firmly entrenched in our hearts. I don't mind telling you that at the start it wasn't easy. We all thought her most unattractive!! Poor little thing. She had been badly managed and was very dirty on arrival with days of powder or cream on her bottom and not much washing! Her nails were black. All this was very off putting as with S it was all so perfect. The poor little J missed having a bottle of milk or water every one and a half hours which she had been having. She yelled her head off night and day. But gradually she began to improve and now she really is a lovely baby.

She has improved greatly in looks and is very healthy with lovely red cheeks. But her real attraction is that she is always laughing and smiling and is so placid and good natured. I think in the end she will get on better with my husband than he does with S who is very unapproachable and shy at the moment. But we adore her and she is a very pretty child and most intelligent. So thank you Miss C for being so understanding about everything and also for knowing that J would eventually wind herself around us. I do wish you would take a day off and drive down here before the petrol goes and see them both. We'd love to have you.

Please do not think that I am criticising about J when she arrived. I think it is wonderful how all these babies are coped with and looked after and clothed. It must be an awful worry. I was only explaining to you the great odds J had to contend with! She was so ugly.

Happy Christmas to you all. Very many thanks for everything."

My father was diagnosed with terminal cancer just three years after this letter was written. Miss C wrote again to offer her condolences. My mother wrote back "*I am lucky to have the children but we all miss him terribly*" She was a wonderful mother who continued to make me laugh a lot.

My birth parents outlived my adopted parents. All of them owe the Irish Adoption system who rescued me at a time of extraordinary difficulty, a huge debt of gratitude and most of all so do I.

Jane

IMAGES IN YOUR MIND THAT YOU CAN'T EXPLAIN ARE VERY ANNOYING

I remember when I was young I was some place with my Mum and Dad. There were white wall tiles on the wall with drawings on them in the area we were seated. One tile had a little boy dressed in blue eating something. I was told it was written on the tile that he was called Jack Horner. On another there was a girl in blue also who held a stick. She was called Bo Peep. I asked my parents in the years afterwards where the place was. They were unable to recall. I believe it was the time we went to Dublin to collect one of my sisters. I found out years later that it was a famous city centre cafe.

Then there was another time I remember being out with my Dad somewhere. He used to take me out in the morning scouring the countryside looking for fresh mushrooms. I remember one time we were sitting in the car and the day was wet. My Dad gave me a bar of chocolate. It looked big and had a blue wrapper on it. Dad mentioned that I was his son but he was not my "real" father and my mum was not my "real" mum. He explained to me that I was adopted. I thought the chocolate tasted brilliant.

Mum would tell me whenever I would ask about being adopted that I was in a room with lots of other children in white cots and I was the most beautiful baby there. That the minute she saw me she fell in love with me and took me straight away. I have two sisters and they are adoptees also. I think they may have heard the same story.

Forms were very confusing things when growing up. "Where were you born", "County of Origin", "Name of Mother and Father". Feelings of doubt, confusion, disloyalty and guilt started to surface. The way I looked at things was that I had a different start in life from my peers. Still it never really bothered me being adopted. I just had a different start in life that was all. Growing up, education and getting work were bigger priorities.

Then when I was getting married a strange thing happened. Details of my past, my baptismal certificate and possibly my birth certificate were given to the Bishop of the town where I was getting married, passed on to the priest who was doing the ceremony and then back again. I was being circumvented and a lot of people were getting to see personal information about me that I didn't know about. I was not happy about this situation and I expressed at the time that I should be entitled to see my details. I was told candidly that I had no entitlements to see any information about myself.

My wife comes from a large family with a rich history. It made me realise that I had no real tangible history of my own.

When our children were born issues arose and family medical histories were discussed at various points. I always had to mention that I was an adoptee and had no family medical history at all. I decided to try and get as much personal details as I could.

When visiting Dublin at one time I decided to get a copy of my original birth certificate. I went to Joyce House and what I received the long form birth certificate that adoptees get. I enquired and was told that I couldn't get access to my original records. I was frustrated and determined to find a way to get more details. Later I was to discover that I had been renamed after being adopted which would have made the task even harder, if not impossible.

During the 1990's a prominent radio presenter was discussing the issue of adopted persons not being able to access their records and making an issue of it. One day I was in the Dublin city and decided to make enquiries as to accessing my personal records. I eventually got to meet a counsellor and relayed my life story in general up to that point. I was asked what agency I was with. I had no idea so some enquiries were made. I was told that I had been placed by the Catholic Protection and Rescue Society of Ireland now called Cúnamh and located on Anne's Street in Dublin.

At Cúnamh I met a social worker who recalled that she remembered me as I was one of her initial placements. She outlined my birth details and non-identifying particulars concerning my natural mother. It all went over my head at the time I was so anxious, excited and delighted with finally getting some information. She mentioned that my father had kept her informed of various aspects of my life as I was growing up which really surprised me.

Some time afterwards I received documentation officially informing me about my natural mother and where I was born. I didn't, however, get any medical details and as this was one of the main concerns and reasons for my search I was a little disappointed. I was happy that the void was being filled and I was getting some closure. I was asked if I wanted to leave a letter in case someone came calling so they could find me if needed. Thought it unlikely but I did leave a letter anyway.

Then a few years later in 1998 I got a surprise contact letter from Cúnamh. I was asked to call in to discuss additional information regarding my background. I learned that I had a half sister in England who was interested in contacting me. She had been doing her own background search as an adoptee and I came up in the records there too.

My sister came to visit me and meet my family. I discovered from her that I had uncles and cousins living not too far away! I went to visit my uncle and when I met him it was like looking in a mirror. She told me there was another half sister. We eventually tracked her down and we got together one weekend in England.

The resemblances were striking. I also went to visit my uncle and when I met him it was like looking in a mirror.

I met my birth mother in 1999. She was married and has a family. They were surprised when they found out about us. Eventually we met and it was a very emotional time for us all. I have been invited to family events and met more cousins. For the most part it has been a positive experience.

As I am interested in genealogy I started to complete a family tree and in doing so found out a great deal about my background and natural family. My uncle is also interested in it and helps me with information. I know now of hereditary health issues that have caught up with me. I am lucky in that I have had the necessary surgery to rectify it.

I also found out along the way that I had an uncle and cousins not living too far from my Dad's family in the town where I grew up. It really is a small world.

Families fall apart eventually. The people that you knew growing up are scattered and common events are now vague memories. My Dad passed away in 1998 and Mum in 2008. I am very lucky to have had such wonderful parents. Like all families we didn't always see eye-to-eye on everything but I am what I am today because of them. My hope is that they were proud of me and how I turned out.

I am very fortunate in that my history has come back to me. I don't feel alone or disjointed anymore. I now know where I come from and the circumstances that led to me being put up for adoption. I also have a better understanding of my parents and the reasons that led to them adopting me.

One of my sisters mentioned that she felt alone now that the family was broken up. She traced her family and found her birthmother. She is still looking for further information. I have helped my other sister find some family background but she is happy to leave things as they are.

Adoption affects three sets of lives. The current system of personal information access is very difficult and antiquated. There are a lot of unhappy people because of it, adoptees and birth mothers. This is my story.

Mike

In Memory of Elizabeth

"Having a child means a piece of your heart is walking around in the world". Unknown

"I believe it is better to tell the truth than a lie. I believe it is better to be free than a slave and I believe it is better to know than to be ignorant". HL Mencken

"Children and mothers never truly part - bound in the beating of each other's heart...." Charlotte Gray

"There are two different kinds of strength. There's the strength to make a parenting plan and then there's the strength to give that plan to another". Unknown

Yours faithfully

Kathy

It Has Been a Good Year

I always remember as a child our annual Christmas trip to Dublin to buy Christmas presents and to soak up the magical festive atmosphere. The excitement for me and my little brother seeing all the bright fairy lights and decorations, wrapped in about 20 woolly jumpers each. This trip always included a visit to the old building with the great big door, Mam and Dad always liked to pop in to see their social worker and other staff, for a cup of tea and to catch up. I was always fascinated with the building, knowing this was where I had come from. My imagination led me to believe there was a room full of sleeping babies in cots, pink blankets for the girls and blue for the boys, up the winding stairs, for parents to choose from.

With these fond memories in mind, almost 23 years after my adoption my heart finally led me to contact Cúnamh myself. Although this time was medically rather than emotionally motivated. I was looking for medical history information which I needed as I was having some tests done on my heart (all was fine, thank God). I was put in contact with a very helpful and friendly social worker. When I met with her to collect my information, she had two forms in her hands - the first being the basic medical information I had requested, the second all the information they had on file for me. This hadn't entered my thoughts before then but it intrigued me. With nervous anticipation, I took both.

This was the beginning of a new chapter with regards to understanding my past. It was very emotional to read the first few lines, the length of my birth mother's pregnancy, my birth time, weight and head circumference, and then where I was placed in foster care. Irrelevant little details to a non-adopted person but I had never known these little things about myself before. My Mam and Dad were always very open and honest and shared everything they knew of my birth mother and how they got me, but they simply didn't know all the little details. It was very surreal reading it.

Reading on I learned more about myself and my birth mother's circumstances, I began to understand more. My parents were always so positive about adoption and about my birth mother so I never had negative feelings towards her. Up until now I only vaguely knew her story so I could really feel for her reading it. I felt I had only touched the tip of the iceberg and I wanted to know more.

With my social worker's help, and the support of my parents and boyfriend behind me, the first step of contact was put into place, she let my birth mother know I was in touch. All I had to do was wait. It wasn't long before the letters were flowing.

One year on, it has been a rollercoaster for my heart. Receiving the first letter from my birth mother, getting to know her and her children, old photographs, first Christmas card, getting to tell her of my own daughter, my first birthday card. To mark the first year in touch with Cúnamh and my birth mother, I really put my heart to the test; I took part in the sponsored tandem sky dive from 10,000ft! (heart-stopping stuff!!)

It has been a good year, a lot to take in, so I'm taking it slowly. One step at a time, and hopefully some time soon I'll take the next exciting step forward and meet the lady who gave me to my wonderful loving parents (that one's for you Dad!). I finally realise I didn't just come from a room full of babies, on the third floor, of the big old house on South Anne Street.

Christine

A LETTER TO THE SISTER OF MY BIRTH MOTHER

I hope this letter finds you well.

I am writing to firstly introduce myself formally to you. I am Finola and while I was reared in Dublin I am now living in the south of the country as you may have gathered. I was raised as an only child and subsequently realised that I was adopted. In the early 80's I began my search through the agency to trace my birth mother, and, after a long protracted period, I discovered that Ann had given birth to me. She agreed to make contact and we were in correspondence for a few short years. But by this time Ann was unwell, and so, it was difficult. But during our contact we did have many lovely and lively conversations and we exchanged letters, photos and lots of information and anecdotes concerning the family.

An added difficulty for Ann in her communication with me was the fact that her husband did not know about me, and Ann really needed this to be the case. I respected her wishes. I now realise that he died earlier in the year and I know that Ann's anniversary will be soon upon us. She often spoke about you and your own family, and the fact that your mother went to live in Cork having sold the family home in the 70's. Due to this and because you are her only surviving relative in this country (and living at such close proximity), I have often felt that it would be really wonderful to have the opportunity to make your acquaintance.

In recent years I myself fell victim to a diagnosis of breast cancer - a disease that Ann had warned me was prevalent within the family. A serious illness of this nature really does focus the mind and it changes perspectives somewhat it must be said. The sense of unfinished business needing to be attended to has become an increasingly pressing priority for me as a result.

My contact with Ann, my birth mother and your sister, was finished abruptly. Hence, and for obvious reasons, I did not get the chance to close this chapter of my life as I would have liked.

Susannah, (or Susie, as Ann always referred to you), I would ask just one thing of you that would mean such a lot to me - that we could meet, as Ann and I had spoken about so doing. The meeting was to be in Cork at this time of year due to your mother's anniversary. Sadly it was never realised. It never happened. I would ask you now as a tribute to Ann, for us to carry out this intention by arranging a short once-off meeting in order to talk, to share some stories or prayers for her – to very simply honour her memory. An occasion of healing – a closing of the circle as it were.

In what will soon be the 'Season of Goodwill to all', I wish you the many blessings and joys this time of year affords and I would ask you not to disappoint but instead to look favourably on this one small request!

With kind regards,

Finola

LETTER TO JULIA

Dear Julia,

On Thursday, Feb 26th, Nuala was diagnosed with a recurrence of her cancer, this time in her lungs, liver and bones. The consultant could not reassure her that she would have more than a year to live. When this awful news arrived, I felt a powerful urge to contact you and to have you on my side in this crisis. But that couldn't be. Because I am bound, out of love and respect for you, to keep your secret. As I said when I met you, I will do nothing to put that secret in danger.

Nothing in what has been revealed to my birth father's family points in any way to you. As far as they are concerned, you are a nameless woman who met their father in Donegal back in 1955 and that is all there is to it. They also understand and accept that this is a secret which you intend to keep. I have explained to my birth father's family that I cannot tell them who you are. They can see that they have no choice but to accept that. Julia, keep this secret as long as you choose to do so, and please be reassured that I will not put it in danger. But please also remember that you can always pick up the phone and talk to me or to your social worker. We are on your side.

His family were shocked to learn that they had a long-lost brother but their reaction has been amazing. From the first, they showed an overwhelming concern for Nuala and I think that her plight reminds them of the loss of their own mother when they were little children.

It was a great pleasure to attend my sister Nora's surprise birthday party and it was wonderful that all three siblings and their spouses were able to come for our wedding celebration. It was a great weekend.

In the middle of all the thrill and excitement of meeting them, they have always shown great consideration and sympathy for this unknown woman who bears this terrible burden of secrecy. They are very glad to meet me and only sorry that they didn't find out about me earlier. Thank you Julia, very very much for telling me my father's name back in 2005 for that is what has made all this possible. Meeting his family is a prize beyond all price.

Please do not allow yourself to let this get you down. Two months have now gone by since I first met my birth father's family and nothing has changed. Your secret is still as safe as ever. Do not fret, do not be anxious, do not be afraid. Trust me.

While I must remain silent as to who you are, this does not in any way lessen the importance of you in my heart. I am your secret. You are my truth.

Love,

Pádraic

MY STORY

Thirty years ago Ireland was a very different place and the idea of having a child outside of wedlock would have been considered a taboo. Hence, like so many women at the time my biological mother decided to leave the country and head to Scotland to have me where nobody would know her. Having gone full-term I was to be a healthy baby but, unfortunately due to a lack of oxygen at birth, I was born with cerebral palsy. At the time doctors were not sure whether I would survive or not, let alone walk or talk. Thankfully I survived but although my mother had always intended to put me forward for adoption the fact that I would need continuous medical treatment finalised her decision as she felt that this was something that, as a single mother, she would not be able to afford to give me.

Therefore, as I was going to require treatment in the early days of my life, I continued to remain in Scotland for nine months after my birth. As I would not need to spend the whole of this period in hospital I was placed with a foster family in Scotland after my discharge. The family with whom I was placed were really quite good to me and did whatever physiotherapy with me that was necessary. After the nine months had passed the hospital decided that I was fit enough to travel so, at my mother's request I was returned to Ireland for fostering with a hope that I would eventually be placed with a couple for adoption.

Being escorted to Ireland by a social worker I was to be placed once again with another foster family. At nine months old I was much older than the babies that this family were used to fostering as most of them were usually gone for adoption by the time they were six weeks. In addition to this, having been told that I was disabled, they were nervous to begin with as they weren't sure of what I would be capable of doing. Hence, when I sat up in the pram and said "Dada" in a pure Scots accent they were both relieved and surprised. The fact that I was nine months old and I had a disability made it difficult to place me for adoption, as most couples want a new-born healthy baby that they can raise as their own. Therefore, while my stay with this family was to be short-term, it became permanent as both the parents and their own family of five children fell in love with me so much that they fought to adopt me, despite being over the age limit which couples are supposed to be when applying to adopt a child.

In 1981 at just gone two and half years of age my adoption became official. After this one of the things that concerned my adoptive mam was how and when she should tell me I was adopted. Speaking to the social worker about it she was told that a situation would present itself when she herself would know it was the right time and this advice was very true. One day after having been visiting my adoptive grandmother, who lived beside Dublin Airport, I came home quite excited about seeing an aeroplane flying over the house. When I told my Mam that I wanted to go on a plane when I was older, she decided that this was the perfect opportunity to tell me that I was adopted and had already been on a plane when I travelled to Ireland. Distinctly remembering been told that my Mam couldn't afford to keep me and wanted me to have two parents, being adopted and chosen to be kept is something I thought was special and took great pride in telling people as a child.

Unfortunately, this changed as I came into adolescence and began to question my identity. Having been informed that my parents were Trinity College students, I put myself under immense pressure to do well in school so that they would be proud of me. While I always knew that there was a possibility that my biological mother wouldn't want to see me it never crossed my mind that this would be the case. Having got involved in swimming and karate as a child and won trophies for various competitions in the sport, my main reason for wanting to have a reunion with my birth mother was so that I could show her what I had achieved despite my disability.

Hence, with the support of my adoptive parents, who were also eager for me to meet my biological mother, I carried out my first search when I was nearly eighteen. Being informed that a lot of the information I had was wrong and being refused a reunion by her were things I found hard to deal with. As an adopted child you are denied access to the information about yourself and where you come from that most other people just take for granted. This was not the only search though that I carried out. A few years ago having a medical problem, I decided to approach the society once again for them to contact her, to see if there was any medical history I should be aware of.

While things worked out fine from a medical point of view she did reject me once again and had the social worker promise I would not try and make contact again. Acknowledging the fact that her life may have changed and she is within her rights to refuse to see me, it still did not make the situation any easier for me to deal with. To be honest I was devastated by the whole thing and together with the fact that I had been bullied and suffered anorexia when I was younger resulted in me spending a number of years in counselling. Now though, with the combination of having reconnected with the foster family in Scotland and being helped and supported by my loving family and partner, I have now begun to accept the situation and move on with my life.

The following is a poem I wrote for my adoptive Mother when I was younger. To me it sums up what being a mother is all about.

A mother is the one, who loves trusts and supports you in everything you do,
although she may not have given birth to you she loves you just the same.

Your first day at school is just as scary for her as it is for you,
For her little girl is taking her first step towards independence.

The years fly by and before you know where you are you are in
those terrible teens,
With those moods swing and hormones flying in all directions,
but she is there just the same sharing in your joy and in your
pain.

She is there to share in the joy of your first love and comfort
you when you suffer your first broken heart, though you may
not always take her advice you know deep down in your heart
she may be right.

Even when you feel you haven't got a friend in the world, a
mother is always there to listen.

A mother is just a name given to a woman who devotes her life
to loving and caring for another.

Anna

My True Family

For as long as I can possibly remember I have been Anthony and even though I'm not her biological son my adoptive mother has treated me like a son, just like I was her own flesh and blood and in my opinion, I am. I mean yes it's true and I'm sure everyone who's been adopted has at one point in their lives thought about their real parents.

For me I know in my heart who my parents are, biology doesn't matter, as for all intents and purposes they are my true family and my true flesh and blood.

Anthony

LIVING IN THE PAST

My mother has started
Living in the past,
A place she has inhabited
These eighty-five years.
As she says herself,
It's hard to believe where
All those years have gone.
When she reminisces,
It can sometimes be
So hard to bear: she
Speaks of me in such
Complimentary terms
That I do not recognise myself.
When you reach the age I am,
It's hard to be told that you are
The best wee boy in the world.

I do not think that either
Of us can understand
How old we actually are.
Sometimes, listening to her,
We are still the couple
Who walked the roads
Together, fulfilling each
Other's dreams: I am ten
Years old, she is fifty,
And there is nothing between us.
So - what is it to be
Proud of your child?
How long does it take
For a mother to be proud
Of her son before he
Becomes proud of his mother?

Pádraic

AG SCAOILEADH

Is tú mo pheaca, a deir sí
Is tú mo ghnímh danartha
Cruthaithe
Agus
Séanta
Cailín mo chléibh
Lig dom tú
a fheiscint
ar nós ribín
ceangailte
le do chraobh.

Jacqueline Finola Gwen

RELEASING

You are my sin, she said
You are my dark deed
Created
and
Denied
My darling girl
Now
Let me tie you like
a ribbon
on our oak tree.

Jacqueline Finola Gwen

Note: writer would like it acknowledged that these poems were conceived or "cumatha" in Irish. The English versions are adapted and translated from the original Gaeilge.

PEOPLE SAY WE HAVE THE SAME EYES

As I sit here on the Sea of Galilee, having just swam in its warm waters, I can look back on my journey/sojourn...my life began in the mid-fifties back in Ireland's green fields. Those concerned with my here-coming, their facial expressions, age and other such details, were to elude my knowledge, for more than half a century.

In my teens I had a curiosity about my natural mum, as I had been told, at a young age, that I had been adopted. This unknowingness stayed with me throughout my teens, and increased as I got older. At times it would subside, but reappear even stronger, than previous, to my dismay.

In my mid-twenties, I discovered some information regarding my birth mum. This led my curiosity down a deeper vain of intensity or desire to know more...I had emigrated in my twenties, working in Europe as a chef, so on my return to Ireland for hols or such, I would look through old birth, death, and marriage records in the hope of uncovering some details of my past, this was a very frustrating period. But it also made me more determined, to get to the answers I sought.

My thirties didn't turn up any news of my pre-parent(s). It was like a maze, the maze became a garden, the garden became a forest and in time it led me into the mountains. In whatever I did or wherever I went, this unknowingness followed me. I was like the character from a Hermann Hesse novel. A lone wolf, roaming around even biting the hand that fed one. Still I marched onwards, always asking and enquiring about the elusive motherhead.

In my forties I returned to Ireland. My adopted parents (whom I would class as equals of my natural parents) were deceased and

I felt that I should try to locate my mum. Surely I could succeed now, I thought, at my life quest…Years went by and still no joy. It was omni present, omnipotent and always on my mind. I had my mind on my mother and my mother on my mind.

The big five o came and went and I knew I had no option but give up. I knew it would drive me mad to continue my quest and at the same time, I knew I would have no ease till I knew the truth. Since coming back to live in Ireland I had got involved with going to Lourdes with my local parish and had done my share of crying for a miracle.

I was about two years into my fifties when I was contacted by Cúnamh to say my mum was in touch. We were reunited and I am a new man, people even say we have the same eyes…It's great.

Roger

THE ADOPTION THAT WENT WRONG

I am writing this piece to show that most times adoption works but sometimes it can go wrong, like mine.

I did not know anything about my past, until Cúnamh traced the history of my family in 2003. I had been trying myself for years and got nowhere but Cúnamh did a wonderful job for me.

I was born in 1929 to a single mother and I was looked after by nuns for a while. I was sent out to several foster parents for two years. Then my mother was put in touch with Cúnamh in 1931.

Cúnamh then found me a permanent foster home with a nice family. This family also adopted another boy and as we grew up we were like brothers. We had some form of Adoption because in 1931 there was no legal adoption. We both took the family's name, but we did not know we were adopted until much later.

I was very happy with this family. I went to school and did quite well. I also made many friends. My foster mother took me to England to see her son, and that's when things started to go wrong.

I was eight years of age then, I was given several versions why I was taken away from my adopted parents, but the one I think was the right one was because my mother took me to England without informing Cúnamh. When we came back from England, we had a visit from a social worker from Cúnamh, then I was taken to court and I was wrongly accused of seeking alms. I did not even know what it meant at that age. I was sentenced to seven and a half years in Carriglea Industrial School at eight and a half years old.

In desperation my foster father even wrote to a T.D. to try and save me from going to Carriglea, he even got the head teacher from my school to write to the court. My foster parents even agreed to keep me without any payment, but nobody took any notice. I was taken away from my parents, heartbroken. I paid a very heavy price.

My adoption had worked up to the time I was eight and a half years old. Then it all fell apart. I was treated like a criminal and given eight years in Carriglea jail.

I know those things would not happen today – or I hope it would not, because I paid a big price for doing nothing and I was not even asked what I wanted.

So that is my adoption experience which was not very good.

I was always worried about my criminal record and I wrote to the President of Ireland for a written pardon. She sent my request to the Minister of Justice and at eighty-one years of age I have received my written pardon.

Kevin

To My Daughter June

The first chapter of my life story is so different to that of yours. You were born in Holles Street Hospital on a freezing November morning. Your nana, Mary, held my hand as you were born, while your Granddad, Tom, and Auntie Majella paced the corridors in anticipation. Sadly, 10 months earlier your Uncle Kenneth had died in a car accident (but we all knew he was there in spirit).

Our family had been torn apart by Kenneth's death and now as we all fought each other to hold you in our arms, the love and hope that we shared for your future lifetime was evident by the tears that flowed silently.

In total contrast my story begins in December 1979. I am four weeks old and your Uncle Kenneth, aged 22 months, arrives into the Adoption Nursery and chooses me as his baby sister. Little is known about the first 4 weeks of my life, that doesn't matter, I have a mam, a dad, a big brother and not long after a little sister to call my family.

After much debate I'm named Jayne Marie. I have dark curly hair, with big brown eyes and beautiful sallow skin. Even though I don't look anything like my adoptive family, I am loved and cherished as every child should be. Growing up I always knew I was adopted. It was never an issue or a problem. It was simply a fact of life. I even had a friend who had been adopted too.

It was probably around the age of sixteen and the age of rebellion that my curiosity began to grow.

My questions were simple –
- Who did I look like?
- Where did my biological family live?
- Had my biological parents married and did I have any other siblings?

As this curiosity grew I started to look at women on buses and trains who looked a little like me and wondered if that could be "her". I shared my feelings with your Nana, she was so supportive and understanding. I think she had been anticipating this question for a long time. And so began the quest.

The first letter I received from Cúnamh explained that my biological mother was young, single and didn't have the money or the support to raise a child on her own. She felt that the best option was to put me up for adoption. For a long time, I was satisfied with this information and it wasn't until you were born that my interest in "her" began to raise its head again. After many discussions and debates, I made a decision that I was going to try and contact "her".

I wasn't expecting the process to take as long as it did, but eventually the letter that I had written in my mind on many occasions was finally in my hand. It was a letter from "her". The letter was simple, it didn't give me a huge insight into what she was like but that didn't matter, finally I had made contact. I replied immediately, telling her all about us and including photographs of the life I had led and the life she had missed out on. I don't know why but I had thought the photos of you and I would have melted "her" heart and she would come rushing to Dublin to greet us with open arms. Life is not like the movies.

We wrote back and forth to one another for a couple of months, sharing little snippets of our lives. I thought that we were getting on well until I received a letter from "her" saying she didn't want any more contact. It was over. I was devastated, she gave me no reasons why, no explanation. It was simply that she did not want to pursue a relationship with me. My heart was broken and I felt abandoned, deserted and dumped for the second time in my life. Finding it very hard to come to terms with this rejection I had a nervous breakdown.

Thankfully our family network is strong, the love and support I received was extraordinary and with lots of encouragement and prayers from Nana Mary, I made it through the dark days.

Life continued and we all moved onto the next chapter in our lives. This was the most unexpected one yet. When the letter arrived from Cúnamh the signature envelope that once brought excitement and anticipation now brought worry and concern. I opened the letter and read it over and over again. This had to be a mistake; she had told me she had no other children. I was the one and only. Yet Cúnamh's letter said something totally different. I had a biological sister and she wanted to meet me. Our meeting was emotional. We talked, we laughed, we cried, we shared our stories. We became great friends.

Thinking back to when you first met Auntie Maeve, you were only 7 years old. There is one single comment you made that I will never forget. You said, "Mam, you and Maeve have the same hands. That's weird". We both smiled at one another but that comment meant the world to me. I belonged.

June, we all have a journey to take and mine has led me to you. You will never know how much I love you. You have changed my life and given me strength and hope at times when I had none.

To Mam, Dad, Ken & Majella – Thank you for all the constant love and support. Couldn't have done it all without you.

To "her" – Why?

Love Ya June Baby,

Your Mam, Jayne

IMAGINE NOT KNOWING!

Close your eyes and imagine seeing your mother's face for the first time. Imagine hearing her voice, smelling her skin, touching her hand. Imagine resting your head on her chest. The feelings that you have in imagining that first time are often the fantasy that an adopted person will play out in their mind as they wish and hope for a meeting with their birth mother. This need to know, this desire to belong is primal. The need to recognize kinship through shared history – is nature at its most primal, nature at its most fundamental.

Imagine what it would be like to have never seen an ear, nose, eyes, even feet, that looked like your own. A sense of identity and belonging is so often linked to physical sameness. 'You look the image of your great Aunt'. 'You look so like your Mum was at your age'. These are words that an adopted person never hears and believes. If and when they are spoken its usually by someone who is not aware of the fact that you are adopted. Then the classic dilemma presents itself – do I say, "well I could not look like her because..." and launch into your often long-winded life journey? Or, do you nod and agree while secretly smiling because you do look like her but are not blood-related?

The challenge of 'not knowing' and the desire to know is at the heart of an adopted person's wish, sometimes even their need, to place themselves in a defined known context – where do I come from? Who do I come from? These are fundamental human questions that the rest of the world simply never has the need to ask.

This wanting to know then gets wrapped up in a complex web of emotions. First there is the feeling of betrayal. A feeling that you are betraying your adoptive family or that they will feel betrayed by you and your need to know. Then comes fear – the fear of the unknown – what if when you find out who and where you came from, when you see your blood relatives, what if you don't like them? What if you don't want to know them? What if you don't even look like them at all?

For me the seminal portrayal of adoption and the dilemma that the need to know gives rise to is the film 'Secrets & Lies'. This film best portrays the search, the meeting, the difficulty in building a relationship and gaining a shared understanding between a birth mother and her adopted daughter. It is challenging and moving and ultimately uplifting, giving voice to what is very often a harrowing journey of self-discovery for both parties.

For me knowing my place of origin in this world was always a challenge. For years I knew nothing of the circumstances of my birth. All I knew was the city – Cork!! But, where in Cork, at what time – was it day or night, was it an easy or difficult birth, how did my birth mother feel, was she totally alone, did she have a sister, a friend in the next room to support and comfort her? The date was not even 100% certain – two different dates in two different documents! How long did I stay with my birth mother, was I an easy or difficult baby – all a mystery. Hidden in layers of Secrets & Lies.

I wanted to know. I believed I was entitled to know and that through knowing who and where I came from I would be able to move forward with my life. I learned from Cúnamh that I was one of the longest 'searchers' writing my first letter of enquiry in secret, under the bedclothes on Belvedere Bond notepaper in 1986!

I am now a 40-year-old gay woman with a birth family and an adoptive family. My journey was long and complicated. There were many twists and turns and tears. I spent days in Lombard Street doing my own research. I spent countless hours with the staff in Cúnamh who helped me in as much as they could given the rules and restrictions that they labour under. My birth mother was the owner of all of the information that I was seeking and it took years for her to give that information, to share that information with me. My story was complicated but what adopted person's story is not?

There were some landmark days on my journey. The first was when I met and looked into the eyes of my birth sister who was also given for adoption. The next was years later when I met my birth mother and later still my birth father; I would describe my emotions on these days as a cocktail of anticipation, fear, awe and moments of pure joy. On those days all my imagining of eyes and ears and hands and all my wondering about how similar we might be, dissolved in the face of the reality of my own flesh and blood.

What have I gained from this journey? A sister – never did I imagine that there might be two of us, born not too far apart, on the same journey. A feeling of completeness – that the jigsaw has been completed and the search is over. With journey's end comes a great feeling of contentment and peace.

Nicola

Wrapped in a bright yellow blanket

You wrapped me in a bright yellow blanket,
The day you gave me away.
Every knitted stitch in making it,
A tear was shed,
Every purl and loop,
A kiss for me,
On mornings when I wouldn't be there for you to
hold and hug each day.
Only we know our story, of our missing years,
Only we have the wish to find missing smiles and lost moments.
Today is a different day,
Of a bond nobody could break,
Today is a reunion that you and I can make.
The dreams and hopes become reality when I hear your voice,
and laugh, the smile and for the thanks and blessing
To those who helped to bring us back together,
To allow us share the childhood apart, the motherhood lost.
The hardest decision you ever had to make has come full circle
And we reunite as family from the cold like being wrapped in
a blanket.

N

OTHERS SHARE THEIR ADOPTION STORIES

LONG AGO

Life was very different in 1956 when I was appointed as Junior Social Worker to the Catholic Protection & Rescue Society of Ireland – the name in itself would indicate a different era. The Society subsequently used the abbreviated version – the initials – C.P.R.S.I. as its title – more acceptable – it rolled more easily off the tongue. It wasn't until the 1990's that the name was changed to Cúnamh – an Irish word meaning help as in "Le Cúnamh Dé". It summed up the aims of the Society – to provide help and care to the children offered for adoption and to their mothers who felt it necessary to make an adoption decision.

My job initially was to visit the children in foster care, mostly babies awaiting adoption, or a decision by the mother as to her choice for the child's future. The majority of foster homes were of a temporary, short-term nature and scattered around Dublin and North County Wicklow. The homes were visited approximately every six weeks. The foster mothers were marvellous women, all with families of their own, who provided maternal love and stability for each baby in those early formative weeks or months. They were paid a subsistence allowance, in 1956 it was £3.10 shillings a month. The foster families were always sad when a child was removed but they accepted that their role was temporary and the baby's future life was with his mother or with adoptive parents.

Prior to my appointment, Miss O'Beirne – I never knew her Christian name – things were more formal then though no less friendly, made the inspections in the Wicklow area. She took her bicycle on the train to Greystones and cycled around the area. She was very well liked and many foster mothers inquired fondly and nostalgically for her when I took over. I had it easier. I drove to each house, many in the shadow of the Sugar Loaf. I really appreciated the scenery and the slow pace of life, having previously worked in industrial Belfast. The Dublin foster homes were different – the pace of life certainly so – but there was genuine goodwill and concern for the babies in all the foster homes.

Another aspect of my work, in those early years, was the preparation of documents for the Adoption Board. The Adoption Act 1952 came on the Statute Books in 1953. Very many children had been placed for informal adoption, but prior to that date, the adopters had no legal rights. Indeed back to the 1920's, 30's and 40's informal adoptions had taken place. The Society saw its function as enabling those parents to avail of the benefits of legal adoption. This required an enormous amount of work – mainly in locating the birth mother of each child to obtain her consent, perhaps many years after the child's birth. In those days there was a veil of secrecy about having a child outside marriage, and for many women the re-opening of this trauma so many years on was shattering and unnerving. Many mothers could not be located and provided sufficient proof was submitted to the Adoption Board of the unsuccessful efforts made to trace her, the mother's consent could be dispensed. Naturally all the birth mothers would have given the Society permission to place their children initially, but a legal Adoption Order required a birth mother's sworn legal consent. The backlog of Legal Adoption Applications was not cleared for several years.

Another very important part of my work in the 1960's and into the 1970's was "Repatriation". The young pregnant woman of that time saw the solution of her problem as flight to England, to avoid the real or perceived wrath of her parents and community. The idea of confiding in parents was rarely considered.

The C.P.R.S.I. had an arrangement with similar organisations in England to provide help to Irish girls, willing to return to their own country. Many girls agreed, on our promise of complete confidentiality and an assurance that their "secret" would not be divulged. This was an absolute condition of their return and completely adhered to by the Society. In the light of today's attitudes this might seem extraordinary or even deceitful, but as already said, times were different – a fact, not an excuse. Why were they encouraged to return? The English Societies were not equipped to cater for the influx of "P.F.I's"! (Pregnant from Ireland). The promise of adoption was guaranteed by us, if this was the mother's wish, but in the mid-20th century there was little other alternative.

Another employee of those early years was Mrs Murphy or "Murphs" as she was affectionately known. A wonderful woman, she joined the staff in 1931 when Mrs Esmonde-White, the Society's first Secretary was in charge and remained until her death in 1977. She was an "escort", that is she provided an accompanying service to mothers and babies. She was the soul of discretion and played a vital role in the work of repatriation. I had the privilege of working with her for over 20 years, so there is a link, however tenuous, from the formation of the Society to close to the end of the 20th century!

It may be hard to visualise now that in those early years, there were more children for adoption than there were parents to adopt them. The concept of childless couples building their family through adoption was new, but the security provided by legal adoption encouraged couples to fulfil their desire for a family in this way. To quote a little verse which sums up the adoption experience for those couples:

> *Not flesh of my flesh,*
> *Nor bone of my bone,*
> *But still miraculously my own.*
> *Never forget for a single minute,*
> *You did not grow under my heart,*
> *But in it.*

During the 1960's, 70's and 80's adoption placements increased enormously. The decline came in the 1990's with the general willingness of grandparents to welcome the birth of a baby to an unmarried daughter, and the greater social acceptance of births outside marriage.

A.R.

A MOMENT IN TIME

It was one of those perfect spring mornings when you feel glad to be alive. As I locked the car my eyes were drawn upwards by the sunshine breaking through the fresh green uncurling leaves, a reminder of new life and of the earth once again renewing itself.

I walked up the tiled path to the hall door and rang the bell. As I waited I was aware of my heart pounding in my chest. Eventually the door was opened. She stood there with her month-old baby boy asleep in her arms, his head resting gently on her left shoulder, his face in close to her neck, her long blonde hair lay in caressing strands across his cheeks. She said nothing. She had already said all that was needed. I followed her up the stairs to the small attic flat they had shared for the previous four weeks. She went and stood by the window indicating the two plastic bags carefully packed for his journey.

Once I had put the bags in the car I arranged the Moses basket carefully, placing it behind the front passenger seat perpendicular to the back seat, I moved the seat backwards to lock the Moses basket into place as best I could. I checked the inside of the basket where the hot water bottle was keeping the blankets warm. I was annoyed that the sheets were pink, they should have been blue.

I went back upstairs, stood and waited. Eventually she nodded that she was ready and she placed her baby in my arms. She indicated that she would not come back downstairs with me. I walked down the stairs with this tiny baby in my arms. I placed him ever so gently in the car aware that his mother was probably looking out from the tiny garret window upstairs. Once I was satisfied that the baby was settled as comfortably and safely as possible I sat into the driver's seat.

As I moved out into the traffic I turned on the radio thinking that the baby might appreciate the "normal sounds" and I am sure also to distract myself. A new pop song was on the radio, it had a quirky beat for its time. I drove away trying not to think of the mother upstairs as I listened to that song about a person being always found "in a kitchen at parties".

That was thirty-two years ago. I do not know where the lives of that mother or that little boy, whose lives together were so abruptly separated on that beautiful spring morning, brought them. There are many prompts in my life to remind me of them both, each new spring when I see the leaves uncurl on the trees, I think of them. I regularly pass that Victorian house where in that small flat under the attic roof a young mother hoped and dreamt of the life she would have with her first-born son. I know I will be reminded at these times because these are constant reminders. I am however, always caught unawares, when, in the unlikeliest of places, I hear the opening bars of a song that still sounds quirky today. I remember, for I too am caught, frozen in that moment in time.

Anne

THE INFANT CAR SEAT

The infant car seat sat securely in my small car. It remained there for much of the time while I was a young social worker in Cúnamh. I was entrusted with the responsibility to counsel women who were experiencing a crisis pregnancy and to visit the foster families who were caring for the infants and young children. The foster families provided care for infants for six to eight weeks after birth in order to give a mother time and breathing space to make a decision for herself and her child.

I recall one mother, who I shall call Mary. She had requested temporary foster care for her infant in order to help her to make a decision for her child's future. On the day she and her baby were discharged, I met her at the maternity hospital, one cold spring morning. The midwife carried her infant down the stairs of the hospital, as it was the policy of the hospital at that time for the nurse to carry the baby down the stairs for fear that a new mother would fall while carrying her child. Mary and I walked together to my car. She had packed a bag of clothes and toys for her child and she helped to place her sleeping infant gently in the car seat. I had asked her would she like to come with me to the foster family, but she felt it would be too much to cope with on that particular day. I sensed her deep sadness. She had the foster family's address and she would visit her baby another day. On that particular day, she just wanted to go home. She needed some time to think and we had arranged to meet a few days later.

I drove her tiny infant to the foster family, carefully navigating through the busy streets of Dublin. During the journey I looked over several times, while stopped at traffic lights, at her baby sleeping peacefully. The foster family welcomed her small baby and they cared for him over the following weeks. Mary visited her baby several times while he was in foster care. The first time she decided to visit the foster family with me and then she visited her baby by herself on other occasions afterwards.

She eventually chose to place her baby for adoption feeling that adoption gave her child the best possibility for a secure and happy future. Yet, I will never forget and I guess neither will she, the day she placed her sleeping infant gently in a car seat.

Mary

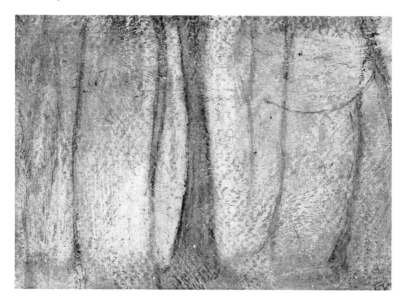

HOLDING HANDS

She cried
He cried
Both just seventeen
Holding hands

What to do?
Who to tell?
Parents
School
Panic, fear
So young
Holding hands

Courage
Mum and Dad know
Relief
Tears
Warmth
Holding hands

Hospital bed
Pink blanket
Tiny hands
Tiny feet
Cannot bring her home
Holding hands

Smiles
Tears
Foster care
Visits
Joy
Memories
Goodbye
Holding hands

New parents
Do not judge
Welcome responsibility
Promise to keep in touch
Will tell her we love her and
Hold her hand

Siobháin

VANISHING STAPLERS

The six years that I spent working in the office in Cúnamh in South Anne Street leaves me with a long list of memories. I witnessed the joy of adoptions; the pleasure of seeing reunions that turned out well; I enjoyed meeting foster parents whose selfless work was always admirable. However, when I think of Cúnamh, I also think of mysterious disappearing stapling machines. Working in that office also ensured that so many of my diets crashed under the weight of Marks & Spencer's best cream sponges.

Vanishing staplers were a constant problem. I had to put my name on mine. Social Workers love staplers, particularly other people's. The office staff occupied the ground floor and the social workers were on the second and third floors. I was very fit when I worked there, I had to be, because I ran up and down forty stairs at least twice a morning chasing my stapler! That fitness didn't come easily, because at Cúnamh it was always someone's birthday. Diets would go out the window as we tucked into lemon drizzle sponges or chocolate gateaux.

My day-to-day work involved putting on headphones and transcribing social workers notes from a Dictaphone. There was never any sameness about the stories. Each day we were transported to another world where sadness, hope and joy mingled on each tape - people longing for a baby to adopt, others looking for their birth mothers and birth mothers trying to make contact with the child given up many years earlier, but not forgotten.

Then there were the reunions. There was a special atmosphere on those days. The biscuit tin would be refilled with fresh biscuits, the stale fig rolls flung into the bin, stocks of tea and coffee checked and at least two cartons of milk bought. Tea is the healing balm of reunions. I've seen three and four cups of tea taken by both parties during an hour-long reunion.

When I wasn't chasing my stapler or eating cake, I loved talking to people on the phone. In one day you could speak to a woman hoping to adopt a baby, a man or woman placed for adoption seeking out their roots, or a birth mother asking, as one woman memorably did *"Has he been looking for me? If he has, could you tell him I still have his little blue blanket. His father and I were very young and didn't know what else to do at the time. We married two years after he was born, but we never had another child."*

Then there were the callers to the door in South Anne Street bringing their children in to see the staff. One little fellow in particular, I'll call him Ben, used to come in with his mam whenever she was in Grafton Street. He'd make a beeline for my desk. I'd always have a special biscuit for him. He'd chat away telling me all his news, a happy little boy. This is the positive side of adoption, giving a child a secure home and a good life.

Val

THOUGHTS FROM A FOSTER FAMILY

We are privileged to have been involved in fostering and adoption for ten wonderful years.

We have met some incredible people and most gorgeous babies.

When friends and family discovered what we were doing, we faced mixed reactions and many questions, with the most common being, "how will you give them up?"

After our first baby went off happy and smiling to his new family, the question for me became "how could we not?"

When you see the sheer happiness that this baby gave to the couple, I personally felt huge guilt, I had three happy, healthy children and I had been honoured to have had time to love, bond and experience this wonderful little human. I only wished I could have given the couple more.

No degree, masters or doctorate could have included the experiences and the emotions we have encountered. From the total helplessness of an underweight baby, to the sheer strength of character of a birth family.

I can hand on heart say that I have loved and still do love each and every little baby that has come into our home.

It has been a very emotional ride, with ecstatic highs and thundering lows, but above all an experience that I would not swap for the world.

We have been so lucky to have had shared all these unique experiences and milestones with our beautiful foster babies.

We have loved you all, very much and wish you all the very best forever and always. You deserve nothing less.

K

HE LOOKS LIKE MY BROTHER

We live through our childhoods with the inherent subconscious expectation that our parents will protect us from everything that's bad in the world. There's no bogeyman in the closet too scary for them, no film so petrifying that it paralyses and leaves the remote control tantalisingly out of reach.

Those of us lucky enough to have parents like that end up seeing them as entirely infallible, omnipotent beings who can overcome any obstacle. Of course, we then hit our teenage years when they are annoying and their desire to protect us really just hems us in, but that doesn't mean that we see them as any less indestructible and invulnerable.

My parents were like that. I had a very happy childhood in rural Ireland, wanted for nothing, loved my parents and felt loved by them. My mother was the boss, ruling not so much with an iron fist as a warm oven mitt – firm, decisive, caring, protective.

I hit my twenties and left home to live in a large European city, returning often home to visit my sister and parents. The protective bubble of home was always there for me, infinitely reassuring and endlessly welcoming.

One sunny June, I came home and we took advantage of the warmth to eat together in the back garden. After dinner, my father and sister took off and left me alone with my mother. I was expecting the usual mild interrogation about my love life, followed by good-natured teasing and giggling.

Instead, my mother was crying. Enormous, sad tears rolling silently down her face, her eyes imploring. I had no idea what was coming, but the sight was already breaking my heart.

When it came, it was a torrent. She spoke for hours. She cried. I cried. We hugged. We spoke some more and cried some more.

She was 28 when she got pregnant. The father disappeared. My mother, knowing that her own mother would have disowned her, packed herself off to a convent for single mothers. Her son was born and taken from her immediately. He was, she was told, adopted by a loving family and was happy. My mother thought she was a terrible person for what had happened. She grew up in an Ireland very different from today, one that, to my eyes, meted out repression through religion, media and government organs. Sex is bad. Woman's place is in the home, supporting a husband. Homosexuals go to hell (if they are even acknowledged to exist). Contraception is illegal.

This atmosphere of fear and authoritarianism is what led my mother to believe that she had to spend over thirty years of her life weighed down by horrible secrets, shame, guilt, self-loathing and denial. I couldn't – can't – comprehend what it must have been like for her. Keeping it from her husband. From her children, that they have a brother somewhere. Her insides must have twisted into a thirty-year knot.

Worst of all, she genuinely feared rejection from my sister and I, that we would judge her and cast her aside. Our responses, ones of love and acceptance, made her cry even harder. When something is buried so so deep inside someone, the effort required to haul it out into the open is gargantuan. Superhuman. When there were no more tears left in either of us, we sat back and looked at each other. She had been building up to this moment for years, and as she sat there in front of me on that flimsy white garden chair, she was depleted.

This woman had managed to give me the impression all through my childhood that there was nothing bad in the world, and that is nothing short of incredible. She herself had undergone one of the most unspeakably horrible experiences that anyone could have to endure, and still managed to get married to a good man, bring up two children and not let a shred of her pain, anger, grief, longing, shame, or guilt in any way touch their lives.

As she slumped, exhausted on that chair, she seemed like the strongest woman in the world.

My father and sister were also told the news, and, with all of our total support, my mother started putting the wheels in motion to let her son know that she would love to see him. Naturally, it's been a difficult road, especially as my mother began dealing with emotions so strongly repressed for such a long time that sorting them out must have been like individually pulling every grain of flour out of a loaf of bread.

They have been exchanging brief correspondence over the past year, my mother and her son. He told us of an extremely happy childhood with two parents who were overjoyed to have him in their lives. He enclosed a photo of his wife and child.

He looks like a good man. A devoted father, a loving husband.

But most of all, despite never having spoken to him or even laid eyes on him beyond that photograph, he looks like my brother.

Steve

COMING HOME

Lost but not forgotten,
ingrained in the psyche of the family,
secrecy, shame, betrayal.

A secret left to die,
but found,
patient and waiting.

Tentative steps,
courage, excitement, joy,
lost but coming home.

Emma

The Journey

It is said that life is a journey and we will all travel many roads with lots of twists and turns and humps and bumps. I have been privileged to travel on a remarkable journey with my husband Nick who was adopted.

I have been married to Nick for 33 years and we are together since I was 16 and he was 20. Not long after we were married in 1978 he often would say to me that he felt different to the rest of his family and that he often felt like he didn't fit in. He was very well-loved and cared for so he couldn't understand why he felt like this. He was the youngest of six and this conversation would come up every so often, then he would put it to the back of his mind. As the years went by and both of his parents died it would still come up for discussion but only with me. In 2003 he was going to be 50 and as he had never seen the long version of his birth certificate he decided he would go and get one. What a major shock he got. He discovered that he was in fact adopted and "The Secret" had been kept from him for 50 years.

He was amazing the way he handled all this. It answered so many questions for him that had been in his head for so long. There were plenty of tears shed around that time but with all the love and support he got from us he gradually got his head around it all. His original birth certificate had his mother's name and address at the time of his birth and his sister had some papers that his adoptive mother had kept regarding his adoption which enabled him to contact Cúnamh.

I think the first day he walked into the Cúnamh office was very difficult for him but he went there to get help and advice. He was treated with kindness and respect and got a lot of information fairly quick regarding the circumstances of his adoption. There was to begin a journey of searching..... With the help and support of a social worker who was assigned to his case he was to continue searching for eight years. His social worker was always there to help and support him in any way she could and we as a family met with her many times.

In July of this year, sadly, Nick's birth mother passed away. He never did get to meet her. It was very sad for him. With the help and support of his social worker he has met his birth mother's brother who is only two years older than him. It was an amazing meeting and very emotional for Nick but a very positive meeting. He has got so much information about his mother and her life both before and after he was born.

He has said that he now feels like the part of his life that was always a mystery to him is now solved. He says it's like the pieces of a jigsaw puzzle had been put together. He is now looking forward to the next chapter in the book of his life. He is a remarkable man who has handled all this with great strength. I am so lucky to be sharing in his journey.........

Trish

To My Mother

She swings through the streets like Cleopatra
Her lips red, her cheekbones high and beautiful
Her bearing is regal, her style immaculate.

She laughs with ease, she cries with sincerity
She loves too much yet does not feel its return.
She holds a secret eating at her being,
A secret she dares not share for shame.

Mum it's ok, a victim of earlier times,
You are loved, respected –
You are Cleopatra.

My mother was placed for adoption in the early 30s and went to live with two amazing people who adored and raised her as their own. They were also wonderful grandparents to all of us. However, her 'giving away' at birth ate at her being and left her with an immense inner sadness which showed in her eyes. Mummy always wanted to trace her birth mother but never did for fear of being disrespectful to her parents, and she has since passed away.

Almost eighty years on from her adoption we have recently found and met with members of her family who didn't know she had existed. It was one of the happiest days of my life, but the happiness was also for her. The concern they showed towards her wellbeing and wanting to know if she had had a happy life was terrific, and at last she had a family which looked like her. She had history.

Looking forward to getting to know my family.

Eileen

THE RAP

Yo yo my name is Joe
I jumped off my seat and
I started to eat
I walked down the street
Then I brushed my teeth
I opened the door and
Somebody shouted four
And that was the score
And they all wanted more

Laura age 9
In honor of her brother who is adopted

"GONE FOR NOW"

Did you ever wonder where I went?
You never come, it's never said
And if I follow will you see
The man I want to be
Cause I, I didn't look but I did find
No, not peace of mind

I know, you don't want to go
And I can feel it was real

The Love you have is gone for now
There's nothing, nothing I can say somehow
The Love you have is gone for now
There's nothing, nothing I can say

Life goes on faces change
Places are new, some things are strange
The same little boy or little girl
That you brought into this world
Has grown, grown without you in their lives
Thought of you a thousand times

The Love you have is gone for now
There's nothing, nothing I can say somehow
The Love you have is gone for now
There's nothing, nothing I can say

You don't have to go
Why won't you stay?
Come on in from the cold
We'll meet again someday

The Love you have is gone for now
There's nothing, nothing I can say somehow
The Love you have is gone for now
And there's so much, so much left to say.

Song written for his dad who is adopted
Stephen

ADOPTION IS LIKE A FLOWER

Adoption is like a flower it starts off as a tiny seed and turns into something wonderful

Aoife
13 year old adopted child

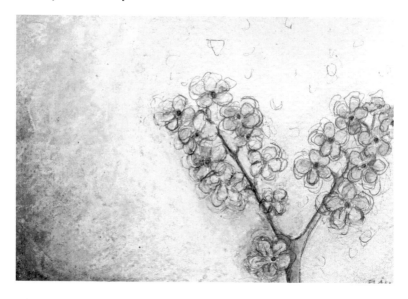